Rediscovering Ghana's Past

Rediscovering Ghana's Past

James Anquandah

Sedco Publishing Limited
P.O. Box No. 2051
Accra
Ghana

Longman Group Limited
Burnt Mill,
Harlow, Essex, U.K.

First published 1982

ISBN 9964 72 024 6 (Sedco)
ISBN 0 582 64309 0 (Longman)

Printed in Great Britain by
Butler & Tanner Ltd, Frome and London

British Library Cataloguing in Publication Data
Anquandah, J.
    Rediscovering Ghana's past.
    1. Man – Prehistory – Ghana
    2. Excavations (Archaeology) – Ghana
    I. Title
    966.7'01   GN865.G/

    ISBN 0 582 64309 0

Contents

List of Illustrations

Maps

Figures and Photographs

Dedicated to C.J., the magnificent

Acknowledgements

I am most grateful to the Ghana National Museums and Monuments Board and the Department of Archaeology of the University of Ghana for permission to make reference to, or illustrate in this book, materials, both published and unpublished. The photographs in the text were all provided by the author and the cover photograph was kindly supplied by Werner forman Archive. Many thanks also to all my colleagues and friends at Legon for their valuable comments and advice, for making available to me research materials (some of them as yet unpublished), or for help in the typing of the manuscript and the preparation of the illustrations. Special mention must be made of Professor Merrick Posnansky, formerly of University of Ghana, Legon, now at U.C.L.A.; Professor and Mrs J. H. Kwabena Nketia, of University of Ghana and U.C.L.A. and above all my wife, Susan Grace Anquandah, for their constant encouragement and moral support. This little book, for whatever it is worth, is a monument to them and to all those countless scholars, technicians and field workers whose sweat and toil have in one way or another helped to produce the materials referred to in these pages.

James Anquandah
1 January, 1980

The publishers are indebted to the following for permission to reproduce copyright material:
Antiquity Publishing Ltd for an extract from 'Archaeology in the Gold Coast' by H. J. Braunholtz in *Antiquity* Vol 10 1936; Oxford University Press for two extracts from *Ashanti* by R. S. Rattray 1923.
We are unable to trace the copyright owner of an extract from 'Diffusionism and Later African Prehistory' by Colin Flight in *Proceedings of the Seventh Pan-African Congress of Prehistory*, 1976, edited by Abebe, Chavaillon and Sutton and an extract from Proceedings of the Seventh Pan-African Congress of Prehistory by R. B. Nunoo and would appreciate any information which would enable us to do so.

Foreword

by Merrick Posnansky

With the appearance of *Rediscovering Ghana's Past*, Ghanaian
archaeology has come of age. At long last the results of numerous
excavations, long hot treks through tangled brush and ten foot high
elephant grass as well as detailed examinations of countless stone flakes
and potsherds by several generations of archaeologists have borne fruit
in this readable account that it is my pleasure to introduce. It is
significant that this achievement has been made possible by James
Anquandah, the first West African to gain a postgraduate qualification
at a West African university. I hope that this book will herald a
succession of other studies on different aspects of Ghana's past by
students trained in the University of Ghana. The book is also a
testimony to the foresighted wisdom of the then University College of
the Gold Coast which in 1951 established a chair in archaeology many
years before any other countries in sub-Saharan Africa. There are still
no chairs in archaeology in tropical Africa outside of West Africa and
one hopes that this book will provide an inspiration for university
authorities elsewhere in Africa to appreciate the importance of
archaeology as a university discipline. Archaeology is not just another
university discipline but has an intangible value in nation building. A
pride in one's past can only be facilitated if one is aware of one's
country's rich cultural heritage. This pride and awareness promote
social and cultural confidence. It is only within the last generation, the
generation of Independence, that Ghanaians have reversed the tide
which threatened to replace indigenous name, dances, art, crafts, music
and festivals by those of Europe. Ghanaian traditional culture was at
best thought of as interesting, though outmoded, and at worst as
'primitive' and 'tribal' by Eurocentric scholars who mostly had little or
no knowledge of the antecedents of that culture. Ghanaian traditional
culture as a result was depreciated by neglect. It is important that
Ghana's history be interpreted by Ghanaians who have a love and
understanding of the culture that nurtured them and their fathers. It is
not inappropriate that Black Africa's first truly independent state in the
twentieth century should have been the first to have established a
university department of archaeology. The impact of the Black Star of
freedom was felt not just in Africa but over the whole of the Black
diaspora. It is my belief that this modest book will have a similar impact
on the transplanted Africans of the New World.
    Archaeology in the past few years has clearly revealed the importance
of the African achievement. An achievement that, contrary to earlier
beliefs, indicates that West Africa had developed metallurgical skills of
a very high order as early as the second millennium B.C.; that towns like

Jenne Jeno in Mali predated the Arab conquest of North Africa by many centuries; that the ancient sculptures in terracotta and alloys of copper stand comparison with the most beautiful creations of the more famous world civilizations; that the megaliths and huge earthen burial mounds of Senegal, besides being unbelievably numerous, betoken the existence of powerful, though still mysterious, chieftaincies nearly two thousand years ago; and perhaps most significantly that the bustling emporia of Ghana were aware of the outside world even if knowledge of them was unknown to the nineteenth-century explorers whose exploits were extolled to generations of West African schoolchildren before the real discovery of Africa began. James Anquandah's book describes Ghana's past within the rich tapestry of West African history and prehistory and will enable future generations of Ghanaians and Africans, both within Africa and the diaspora, to appreciate the excitement of the great and lasting explorations of Africa's past.

James Anquandah makes an important contribution to African historiography in his multidisciplinary approach. For too long there has been a dichotomy in African archaeology between African prehistory concerned with the rather remote Stone Age and the Iron Age treated as a separate entity from the historical period. *Rediscovering Ghana's Past* successfully amalgamates the previously separate periods into a coherent whole which demonstrates the importance of the study of ethnographic data, oral traditions, folklore and linguistics for an understanding of Ghana's undocumented past. Historians will learn from its pages the ways in which the frontiers of historical knowledge can be pushed further back. Ghana is presently suffering from an economic depression, a depression which is, however, not without its silver lining. Deprived of imports rural Ghanaians are again realizing the inherent value of traditional crafts like potting and iron working and turning to their vast inherited knowledge of Ghana's rich natural resources to find locally available functional substitutes for scarce imports like soaps, cooking oils and medicines. Archaeology reveals through time the appropriateness both of traditional technology and of biological knowledge for a successful adaptation to a difficult environment. James Anquandah has provided us with an appreciation of the potential importance of an understanding of that environment and of the resourcefulness of successive generations of Ghanaians. There is still much to learn. Very large areas are as yet archaeologically unexplored. The challenges are there for future scholars to follow the paths blazed within the following pages. I personally feel privileged to have been asked by the author to write this brief foreword for what will certainly come to be regarded as a milestone in the study of Ghana's past. I am proud to have been associated both in the process of the discovery and in the training of the students with whom the author has worked. I wish James Anquandah power to his elbow both as an excavator and educator.

Merrick Posnansky
Professor of History and Anthropology
University of California, Los Angeles   July 1981

1 Introduction

Ex Africa semper aliquid novi – there is always something new coming from Africa. Pliny the elder, who made this statement, was no prophet. Rather, he was a first-century Roman encyclopaedist of science and technology. But his words have been fulfilled down the generations as much in the realms of natural science as in anthropology, archaeology and history.

Nowadays, hardly a month passes by without some notable archaeological or historical discovery being made in some part or other of Africa. These discoveries may range in date from three million years ago to the twentieth century A.D. Remains of early tool-making hominids which have been unearthed recently in various sites in Ethiopia, Kenya, and Tanzania take the story of human evolution in sub-Saharan African back to at least three million years ago. They add to other hominid evidence obtained from areas stretching from Yayo in Tchad to Olduvai in Tanzania and from Ternifine in the Maghreb to Sterkfontein in South Africa. These provide cumulative evidence that Africa has been the scene of all known human evolution from about three million years till about three-quarters of a million years ago when the fully evolved *Homo erectus* man appeared in Asia and Europe. Sir Mortimer Wheeler's memorable statement of nearly two decades ago in *The Dawn of African History* (1961), still holds good:

> Africa may well be the homeland of man . . . . Asia leads the way in human progress; but it is by no means certain that the Garden of Eden, or its more scientific equivalent, should not be located in Africa.

Early man in Africa took important strides in Stone Age technological and other cultural development over a period of some one million years from Acheulean times to the Later Stone Age. Current research in the Nile valley region of Aswan is throwing new light on Later Stone Age hunter-gatherers of the 18th and 19th millennium B.C., whose intensive collecting of barley and other food crops placed them within range of an early adoption of crop domestication. In the regions of the Sahara, and in south and east Africa, picturesque Stone Age works of art have been discovered and studied in the last few decades. Some of them, especially those of the Saharan 'wet neolithic' period are comparable in their conception and execution to Europe's leptolithic murals. In his work entitled *Rock paintings of Tassili* (1963), p. 19, Dominique Lajoux was at a loss how 'to explain the presence on the precipices of Tassili of signs already seen in the rock paintings of the

Atlas, Fezzan, Libya, even of the Spanish Levant . . . running archers, dancing women, representations of wild or domestic animals appear at the entrances of caves or rock shelters . . . . Here and there common stylistic conventions are encountered.'

Scholars of early urban and state development have listed seven regions in the world where urban civilization evolved independently and at quite different times. Yorubaland is listed as one of these primary centres and Egypt as the author of the world's first centralized kingdom. It has been shown that the Biblical Kush of the Candaces was an African state, a legatee of the indigenous gold-rich Kerma culture of the second millennium B.C. At its apogee, Kushite Meroe had a literate and urban civilization which had close commercial, cultural, and in some cases, diplomatic links with the Mediterranean powers of the Near East, Egypt, Greece and Rome. The Zimbabwe hinterland has been shown to be the homeland of an African people who in the early second millennium A.D. raised up a kingdom made famous on account of its gold workings, artistic architecture, and elegant soapstone carvings. It has been established that the makers of Taruga and Nok naturalistic clay sculptures who are also the earliest known iron technologists of sub-Saharan Africa were indigenous Nigerians of the first millennium B.C. It is also known that the masters of Igbo Ukwu and Ile Ife copper and brass technology and of Benin metal and ivory sculptures were indeed indigenous to Nigeria. Besides, archaeological and historical studies have revealed that the early kingdoms of Mauretanian Ghana, Mali, and Songhai were economically viable and literate urban civilizations, as important for African history and historiography as their contemporaries of medieval Christian Nubia and Ethiopia and the medieval Islamic cultures of the east African littoral and the Maghreb. For Africanists, these discoveries and hundreds of others of the last three decades are of more than antiquarian interest. They are of tremendous interest to the historian. Indeed in Africa, where there has been marked continuity of past traditions into modern times, the monuments and traits of the past represent the antecedents of present-day political, social, and economic systems. To denigrate the African past is to the African probably tantamount to a denigration of his extant traditional culture.

Barely a decade and a half ago, Hugh Trevor-Roper, Regius Professor of History at Oxford, could say to his colleagues and students: 'Perhaps in the future, there will be some African history to teach. But at present there is none; there is only the history of the Europeans in Africa. The rest is darkness . . . and darkness is not a subject of history.' (*The Rise of Christian Europe*, 1965, p. 9) Trevor-Roper went on to counsel his fellow countrymen that they could ill afford to 'amuse [themselves] with the unrewarding gyrations of barbarous tribes in picturesque but irrelevant corners of the globe'. A few years ago, Trevor-Roper's view received support from William Ochieng in an article in the *Kenya Review* (1974) entitled, 'Undercivilisation in Black Africa.' 'It will not be enough', said Ochieng, 'just to glorify the African past by lifting shoulder high a few of her glittering achievements like the Zimbabwe architecture, the primitive peasant empires of the Sudan, and the Makonde sculptures . . . mere flashes within a background of utter stagnation'. The poverty and 'darkness' which characterised the approach to history and historiography that existed till only a few decades ago in Africa must be readily admitted. On the other hand, to describe as 'utter stagnation' and 'unrewarding gyrations of barbarous tribes' a people's past whose proper documentation had been delayed for want of the right historical philosophy and techniques sounds extremely prejudicial. It seems to me that the so-called darkness shrouding Africa's past was due essentially to the unavailability, or the late arrival, of modern scientific technology and ideas and modern research methods.

It is thanks largely to European scholars that the foundations of African history and historiography have been laid in the last twenty years. For this, Africa owes much gratitude to Europeans for the collection and description of valuable historical and cultural data. But research entails not just the collection of facts but also interpretation. It is quite clear that in the interpretation of the facts, European thinking has been tainted by a prejudice rendered endemic ever since the Hamitic hypothesis was first postulated. In the first few decades of this century, Harry Johnston and C. G. Seligman propounded and popularised the Hamitic hypothesis in which they described the historical achievement of Africa as the achievements of in-coming pastoral Hamites, quicker-witted and better-armed than the indigenous agricultural negroes whose lands they overran. European scholars working in Africa took their cue from Johnston and Seligman and traced nearly all important cultural developments in Africa either to Asia or Europe, or to the Maghreb or Egypt. There are some who would today regard the mention of the Hamitic myth as tantamount to flogging a dead horse. There is evidence to the contrary. In spite of the revelations of two decades of historical and archaeological research, there is now a sort of neo-Hamitic school which propagates the idea that the basic props of African society – agriculture, metal technology, urbanization, state formation and literacy, were erected on ideas necessarily diffused from external sources. An outstanding example is the current debate on the origins of agriculture, and especially iron technology. For instance, one scholar has stated in the book *Discovering Nigeria's Past* (1975) that:

> the technique of iron smelting and iron working was only
> developed in one area at one period of time and that after it had
> become established in this area, a knowledge of it spread outwards.
> In the case of iron this area was in north-eastern Anatolia, a part of
> Asia Minor where it was invented about 1500 B.C. Whereas iron did
> not become common in Egypt until 600 B.C.

No concrete evidence has been adduced to prove the case for either diffusion, or local invention, of iron technology in Africa and this is nothing but the old idea of *ex oriente lux*, the idea that the light of civilization invariably radiated from the east outwards. Colin Flight, a British archaeologist at the University of Birmingham, England, and former lecturer at the University of Ghana, lamented the persistence of this prejudice when he addressed the seventh session of the *Pan-African Congress of Prehistory* (1971):

The conventional approach to later African prehistory is indeed diffusionist . . . . Diffusionism involves a reliance on null hypotheses in favour of diffusion. It is an approach which allows diffusion the benefit of the doubt. A 'diffusionist' will not admit independent invention unless he is compelled by conclusive evidence to the contrary to abandon his preferred hypothesis. Conversely, the same is true of an 'independent inventionist'. Diffusionism is an approach, an interpretation . . . and the same is true of the Hamitic hypothesis . . . . From the diffusionist point of view, a lack of evidence is not distinguished from evidence for diffusion. Instances of diffusionist thinking are easy enough to find in the literature of the past ten years . . . . If *ad hoc* assumptions are allowed, it seems fair to ask how a diffusionist hypothesis is ever to be proved false. . . . Unintentionally, but inevitably, the diffusionist approach has tended to create the notion – prevalent enough without further encouragement – of Africa as a cultural backwater. Second, it has had the effect of making African prehistory look easy. To suppose, or to be supposing, that later African prehistory is really rather marginal and really rather simple can hardly be to our advantage. (*Proceedings of the Seventh Pan-African Congress of Prehistory,* Addis Ababa, pp. 321–323).

Rediscovering Ghana's Past is primarily an archaeological documentary, which seeks to bring together, in a critical spirit, the scattered and varied information on archaeological discoveries made since the early part of this century and to discuss the efforts of scholars towards a meaningful synthesis of this information. In the figurative sense this book refers also to studies involving the use of other historical resources, such as oral traditions, written records, ethnography, linguistics, and geology. In Ghana, prehistoric building and potting methods are still used in certain parts of the country today. Many arts and crafts and traditional political, social and economic systems, languages and beliefs of the last one thousand years are still extant today. Thus it is not only unwise but manifestly impossible to discuss later prehistory and archaeology without reference to other related subjects.

What is archaeology?

The mention of archaeology immediately conjures up in the minds of some laymen frightful images of messing up old graves and disturbing the rest and peace of burials. It conjures up in others images of unbalanced or restless scholars walking in jungles, looking for lost cities. To such people, the archaeologist is no more than a grave digger or an adventurer. There are others who hold profound admiration for the archaeologist partly because of the array of scientific skills which he employs, or pretends to command, partly because of the fun and the knowledge which he derives from his exploratory travels into strange and unknown places to discover exciting ancient sites. Such people find great excitement in mass media reports on new archaeological discoveries such as the Egyptian Tutankhamun burials, the Meroe and Ballana royals buried with gold jewellery, Islamic stone structures and tombs at Kilwa and Gedi on the East African coast containing Chinese porcelain and Islamic pottery and coins, magnificent Greek and Roman temples, amphitheatres, swimming pools and aqueducts along the North African coast or medieval storied palaces and inscribed tombstones in the West African Sudan.

Archaeology is a behavioural science – the study of the material remains of man's activities in the past. Its documents are largely non-verbal, the artifacts or products of a sequence of human behaviour. Archaeology involves the strict application of scientific methods of excavation, recording, and artifact analysis for the study and explanation of the cultural patterns associated with ancient human artifacts. Some of the research principles and methods employed in archaeology, such as stratification and field surveying, several scientific methods of dating and statistical analyses may be borrowings from other disciplines. Archaeology may also resort to the use of data from related sources of history as aids in archaeological explanation. But, on the whole, the aims and objectives, research approach, and the data which archaeology deals with, distinguish it clearly from any other discipline and make it a subject in its own right.

Archaeologists are often confronted with questions such as: How do you discover your sites in the first-place? How do you carry out the actual excavation? What sort of objects do you find in your excavations? How do you date the objects you discover?

Finding the site

Some archaeological sites in Africa contain large and easily visible structures identifiable even by laymen as belonging to antiquity, for instance, the pyramids of Egypt, the stone obelisks of Aksum, the stone megaliths of Senegal, Gambia, and Mali, and tumuli burial and settlement mounds of northern Ghana, Tchad and Mali. Other sites which are either partially visible above ground or completely invisible at ground level may be discovered either by chance, or when the archaeologist carries out reconnaissance, by walking and observing or by means of photography from an aircraft.

Many sites in Ghana have been discovered through archaeologists walking over the countryside observing and recording. Sometimes they have followed the direction given in European maps. Sometimes they have used oral traditions to locate ancient sites. For instance, the site of Ayawaso, capital of Greater Accra in the seventeenth century, has been discovered in this way. A study of the local vegetation may reveal unusual patterns of plant growth. Often the site of an ancient settlement sustains luxuriant plant growth because of the large quantity of litter piled up over the centuries, thus creating a vegetation pattern which is conspicuously different from the surrounding vegetation. Quite often, though not always, the presence of baobab trees betrays archaeological sites. At the site of the old Dangme town of Ladoku, near Dawhenya dam which the author excavated recently, nearly two hundred baobab trees can be counted in a typical 'gallery woodland savanna' that shows up both in air photographs and to the naked eye in sharp contrast to the surrounding poor savanna scrubland. Sometimes, Ghanaian farmers working in their fields, schoolboys sweeping plots on school grounds, and labourers working in mines and on road, railway, dam, or building constructions suddenly discover the material remains of ancient people. Where they have been educated about the importance of such discoveries, these people report their findings to the nearest museum or school headmaster. Many hundreds of sites were discovered in a series of round-the-year ground surveys and fieldwork which were conducted during the great road-building period that preceded and followed the attainment of Ghana's independence. More recently, the site of Boyase hill, near Kumasi, has been discovered as a result both of chance and the application of science. One day in July 1971, a botany lecturer, Leonard Newton, of the Kumasi University of Science and Technology took off in a Ghana Airways plane from Kumasi Airport, bound for Accra. To his surprise, Newton suddenly saw from the air a number of *Borassus ethiopum* palm trees growing on a hill-top near the runway, some 160 kilometres south of their nearest normal woodland savanna habitat in the Brong Ahafo region. On his return to Kumasi, Newton hacked his way with the help of local guides to the top of this hill located above the village called Boyase. He then found himself on an 'island' of savanna vegetation surrounded by thick forest, and on the hill-top were growing typical savanna plants like the ground orchid.

More surprise awaited him on a later visit when he saw nesting there the standard-winged nightjar, a bird which normally inhabits the savanna further north. Newton recorded many artificially made grooves on the granite outcrops and picked up a number of polished stone axes,

Fig. 1.1 University of Ghana students taking measurements of stratigraphic levels during the Begho excavation, 1975

microliths and potsherds scattered around the ancient ruins of stone mud-and-pole structures. These, and other artifacts, were later identified by archaeologists from the University of Ghana as belonging to the Kintampo culture of Ghana, dated elsewhere to around the mid-second millennium B.C. The site was later excavated by the present author.

Excavation is the heart of archaeology. There is an archaeological maxim that excavation destroys and absolute excavation destroys absolutely. This means that the ancient objects and features are located in the ground in a certain order and pattern in relation to each other and so once they are removed from their context, the evidence of relationship and order is 'destroyed'. This makes it imperative that during excavation all information must be recorded carefully, and that, in any case, no excavation should be undertaken unless it is geared towards answering a specific problem or problems. Excavation entails mapping the site and showing its position within a country and its height and configurations in relation to its surroundings. This requires the use of the methods of a surveyor. The archaeologist may lay out a grid system having east to west and north to south co-ordinates to facilitate an easy three-dimensional measurement of the position of important artifacts in terms of direction and depth (Fig. 1.1). A record is also made of the changes in style of the commoner artifacts such as pottery at different levels in depth. This is important as it provides a means of relative dating for different stratigraphic levels or periods of human occupation, and provides also an indication of changing patterns of trade, human population or culture.

Fig. 1.2 Excavating a 17th-century incinerator by the 'quadrant method' at Ladoku, 1978

Photography is a quick and vivid method of recording archaeological data. Often, artifacts and burials are photographed in their original position within the soil section. Photography also permits the excavator to keep a record of the different phases of the excavation to enable him to remember details when he comes to write an account of the excavation. The archaeologist pays attention to stratification in the site. Stratigraphy is a principle of archaeological excavation borrowed from geology. Say a group of ancient people 'A' lived on a site and left behind their litter. A second group 'B' coming after them built their settlement on top of the remains of the previous settlers. A third group 'C' built on top of the second settlement, and so on. This means that the culture of people 'B' is older than that of 'C' but younger than that of 'A'.

The method used in the actual excavation of a site depends on the type of site – whether a mound or tomb containing human burials with 'grave furniture', or remains of dwellings such as caves, mud huts or stone palaces, or rubbish dumps or protective defences such as earth-

Fig. 1.3 Grinding stones excavated from the incinerator at Ladoku

works (Fig. 1.2). The method used also depends on whether it is a small-scale selective or 'test excavation' or a large-scale 'area' excavation. In a 'test excavation', an archaeologist may merely want to find out the nature of the vertical stratification of a site and so ascertain the relative age of its different units. In an 'area excavation', the archaeologist seeks to strip down a large area not merely to obtain chronological data, but also to find out about the social, political, and economic life of the people.

The types of tool used by the excavator also depend very much on the nature of the materials turning up in the site or the stage of excavation reached at any particular time. Picks and shovels are used to break and remove the top soils. But a mason's trowel becomes the main tool once the diggers enter the main zone of archaeological deposits. In the case of excavating delicate human burial remains, it becomes necessary to use brushes and small knives. The types of tool are also determined by the environment of the site. Whereas trowels, hoes and baskets would suffice in excavating desert sites in Egypt, picks, shovels and wheelbarrows are vital in the excavation of tropical sites. Methods employed in excavating caves or rock-shelters which have limited space may also vary slightly from open-air sites.

The types of object found in excavations in Ghana are determined again by the nature and function of the site in antiquity. A burial site often produces skeletal remains together with pottery, terracotta portraits, ornaments and weapons associated with the burial either as

Fig. 1.4 Excavating a 17th-century midden at Ayawaso (Greater Accra) by the 'trench method'

'furniture' for the life hereafter or as part of the materials for propitiating the dead. An ancient rubbish-dump site may produce remains of food such as bones of animals, molluscs, pottery, grinding stones, metal implements and European imported goods. A house-mound may throw up domestic pottery, ornaments and smoking pipes, and sometimes, the occasional human burial underneath the house floor. A metallurgical workshop site may contain clay crucibles for melting copper or the remains of mud-built furnaces for smelting metals, slag which is the product of iron smelting, industrial pottery, or specimens of finished implements or ornaments. Examples of excavated settlement mounds are Ayawaso and Ladoku in the Accra plains (Figs 1.4 and 1.5). Excavated burial mounds are known from Ahinsan in Asante, Buipe and Daboya in northern Ghana. A variety of metallurgical workshop sites of different periods have been excavated at Begho and Bono Manso in Brong Ahafo and at Achimota, near Accra (Fig. 1.6). Rock-shelters and caves have been excavated at Kintampo, Bono Manso, and Abetifi area.

Methods of dating

A key aim of archaeology is to decipher the vicissitudes of culture over time and space. Sites and their cultural contents can be dated relatively through studies on stratigraphy and analytical studies on pottery and

Fig. 1.5 View of the trench cut to reveal a circular mud incinerator constructed in the 17th century at Ladoku

other cultural material arranged in chronological series and according to types. But this form of dating cannot be given in a number of years. There are two other methods of dating employed regularly in Ghana, namely, cross-cultural dating by association, and radiocarbon dating. These have greater precision and can be given in a number of years. First, cross-cultural dating. If, say, imported foreign pottery or glass bead or a smoking pipe is found within an archaeological layer in association with local cultural materials, and the date of the foreign import is known from its source of origin, then the local cultural materials with which it was associated can be dated in calendar years after due allowance has been made for time elapsed between its manufacture and export and its use within the local setting. Large-scale smoking began in seventeenth-century Ghana when tobacco became an important staple of European trade to west Africa. From about A.D. 1600, Ghanaians began making smoking pipes locally. It has been possible to work out a scheme of types of local smoking pipe for the purpose of dating sites of the period from A.D. 1600 onwards. This has been extremely useful, especially in hinterland sites without direct evidence of foreign imports. Cowrie shells were imported via northern Africa from the Indian ocean islands into West Africa after A.D. 1000. These shells provide useful means of dating sites in Ghana. Beads manufactured in places such as Holland, England, Venice, and Czechoslovakia have been excavated from sites of different dates after A.D. 1500. A comparative study of trade beads has provided a somewhat provisional and uncertain framework for dating sites in Ghana.

Fig. 1.6 The litter of a 17th-century copper and iron smiths' factory at Dwinfuo quarter of Begho with iron bracelet, pottery, and clay crucibles for melting copper (marked by white headed rods) in situ

The radiocarbon method of dating invented by the physicist, W. B. Libby, during atomic research has helped to fill the time-gap between the end of the Later Stone Age and the advent of the bearers of Islamic and European civilization. The basic principle of radiocarbon dating is that all living organisms take in from the atmosphere radioactive carbon, called carbon fourteen, or C14 for short. When an organism dies, it ceases to take in radioactive carbon which therefore begins to decay at a known rate. Half of the total radioactive carbon disappears within about 5730 years and half of the remainder disappears in an equal number of years, and so on. If a specimen of either charcoal, wood or shell in sufficient quantity is found in an archaeological deposit under conditions which show that it has not been contaminated by radiocarbon from modern roots or objects, it can be processed in a radiocarbon laboratory for a date. Most sites belonging to the period between 60 000 B.C. and A.D. 1750 can be dated by this method.

In some hinterland areas certain distinctive types of local pottery which have been reliably dated by radiocarbon, in some contexts can be used as 'guide fossils' for dating approximately, sites in which organic samples are not found. A case in point is the fifteenth- and sixteenth-century Kisoto ceramic which was traded widely in Gonjaland, which has facilitated an understanding of cultural development in the Black Volta and White Volta confluence area. After nearly half a century of archaeological research in Ghana, the first notable achievement of archaeology is the establishment of a fairly reliable, though incomplete, chronological framework of Ghanaian cultural history of the last 3 500 years. The dating of the first three thousand years has been made possible by the application of radiocarbon dating. A fifth of the number of radiocarbon dates relate to Ghana's earliest-known cattle-herding village communities. Most of the rest relate to Iron Age communities and kingdoms from the second century A.D. to the eighteenth century. Radiocarbon dates are not infallible. There is a margin of error attached to every date expressed by a plus or minus. Also, dates obtained for prehistoric periods especially need to be calibrated, that is, corrected, with a sequence developed from tree-ring chronology.

Preservation and analysis of materials

There is a field of archaeology called conservational archaeology. This caters for the scientific preservation of all cultural materials, especially those susceptible to rust and other types of decay. There is usually present among a team of excavators a technician who carries out 'first aid' treatments on human and animal bones, metal or wooden objects found in a fragile state. During the last fifty years, many chemicals have been experimented with for preserving ancient materials. Some archaeological institutions, such as the department at the University of Ghana, Legon, have a conservation laboratory and museum which use modern methods for the preservation of ancient materials. Where artifacts are exhibited in a museum, scientific precautions are taken to forestall any process of disintegration.

The end of an excavation is only the half-way stage in the study of the past of a site. The next stage involves the careful analysis of artifacts found in the individual levels of the deposit and the arrangement of artifacts in classes and types according to their attributes. There was a time when archaeologists spent most of their time in descriptive analysis of artifacts and other data but paid little or no attention to those types of evidence which reveal how ancient people exploited their environmental resources. The 'new archaeology' of our times emphasizes studies aimed at investigating in detail evidence related to hunting, food-gathering, cultivation of crops, cattle-herding, and fishing. The artifacts of the archaeologist have natural as well as cultural features. The natural properties are best studied by means of methods and techniques available to natural scientists and may be expressed in the forms of tables, graphs, mathematical figures, and sometimes even chemical equations. The human properties such as technology and art can be understood and explained by reference to experiences or models known from prehistoric, historical, ethnographic, or modern functional sources.

Archaeologists often seek the aid of various scientific experts in the analysis of their finds. Samples of rock, soils and pottery sherds are studied and reported on by soil scientists and geologists. Such studies may enable the expert to tell whether rock and soil samples were naturally or artificially laid down and under what conditions they were laid down. Tests on thin sections of pottery help to determine the sources of raw materials and technological qualities of the pottery. Botanists may be required to study plant and pollen remains from the site, while anatomists and zoologists may be asked to identify bones and provide information on certain structural details on them. It is thanks to such studies that we now have valuable information on the use, by second millennium B.C. Ghanaian village communities, of oil palm, cowpeas, *canarium* fruit and domesticated cattle, sheep, and goats as sources of food. Metallurgists are sometimes requested to analyse specimens of metalwork, slag, crucibles and fragments of furnace walls found in excavations. Metal experts may carry out analyses of certain metal objects to ascertain technological details such as methods and processes of manufacture and the components of metal objects. Recent laboratory analysis of materials from the excavation of an Akan copper foundry at Begho in Brong Ahafo revealed that the raw material was not from local sources but probably from scraps of metal that were originally parts of imported metal vessels and other objects from Europe (Fig. 1.6).

Excavation is expensive and the money has to be found from some source. Labourers need to be paid for the duration of the excavation which may vary from a few days to several years. Very costly surveying equipment is required for mapping the site so that the exact geographical location of trenches in relation to the general site and in relation to the general district, provincial or national location can be made available to the reader of an archaeological report. Equally expensive are photographic and prospecting equipment and dating by radiocarbon. There are always problems of transporting the research team, excavated materials, and equipment to or from the site. Finance and costing is thus a crucial problem in archaeology. Once the data has been collected and pieced together, the archaeologist is faced with the task of evaluating and interpreting his data. It is necessary to provide the bald facts obtained from research in a form distinct from the excavator's interpretation so that others looking at the same facts can give other interpretations where necessary. It is in the matter of interpretation that the archaeologist needs to have experience or knowledge of models from ethnography or contemporary traditional systems, modern practices, and historical sources.

Every research discipline has methods as well as theories. Archaeology is no different. One subject of archaeological theorising which is crucial to analysis and interpretation of archaeological materials is that of 'culture'. This term is used to describe either man's general material or non-material inheritance or a particular pattern of inheritance. When certain types of past remains, such as pots, implements, ornaments, house forms and burial sites are found recurring in association in a reasonable number of deposits, the group is assumed to be the material representation of 'a people' with a distinct tradition or mode of life. It is on this basis that in Ghana, for instance, we can identify archaeologically the 'Kintampo culture' of the second millennium B.C. (described in chapter 5), or the 'Akan culture' of the period A.D. 1400 to 1800. This concept has its drawbacks, because not all artifacts were laid down in the past, not all are discovered in their original articulated form, not all are even properly identified, and some aspects of everyday life, especially the ideological and sociological aspects, are rarely manifested in artifact form. Thus the proportion of the total cultural context on which archaeology can throw light is limited to the surviving evidence that can be extracted. It is partly because of these limitations in the survival of evidence that archaeology gives the impression of being dependent on other subjects for its effectiveness.

Ethnographic studies

In Ghana, the tropical climate and soils tend generally to promote the preservation of inorganic to a much greater extent than organic artifacts. Sites with the best-preserved materials include those of the last three millennia. Thus archaeologists are always happy to welcome data provided by ethnography, oral traditions, and linguistics. Ethnography which involves the study of contemporary traditional institutions, cultural materials, modes of life, and techniques used in arts and crafts, throws light on what would otherwise be hidden treasures of the past. It is thanks to ethnographic studies conducted by the University of Ghana and the Ghana National Museum in several parts of Ghana, that archaeologists have some insight into the processes of traditional ironworking, traditional pot-making, and traditional cloth-making and building during the last millennium or so.

Oral traditions

In the pre-independence period, historians and archaeologists in Ghana did not realise that oral traditions contain so much valuable data. In recent times, nearly every Iron Age archaeologist has had to resort to oral tradition as an aid to archaeological explanation of cultural development. During the last decade, the Brong region of Ghana has been the scene of intensive collection of oral tradition. Local traditions have been used by scholars in locating the industrial, urban, trade, and capital sites of Bono Manso, one of the earliest kingdoms to emerge in Ghana. Other scholars researching at the famous Brong site of Begho which specialised in international commerce, linking Mali with the Ghana coast, have similarly succeeded in using local traditions in locating and naming the quarters and suburbs of that great township. One archaeologist has employed oral traditions in the attempt to unravel the past of old Wenchi, also in Brong. In southern Ghana, one of the puzzles of archaeology during the last forty years has been the authorship and dating of the numerous earthworks of the Akyem Kotoku area. That the riddle is partly resolved is chiefly due to the application of oral tradition side by side with radiocarbon dating and pottery studies. Archaeological research at Yendi Dabari, New Buipe, Jakpasere, and Daboya, has benefited from parallel research on oral traditions. Along the coast lands, oral tradition is an important element in the current inter-disciplinary archaeological and historical project aimed at unravelling the early history of the Ga and Dangme peoples of the Accra plains (Fig. 1.7).

A number of historians of the University of Ghana have made very important contributions to the documentation of oral history in Ghana, among them, Kwame Daaku who has researched on Gonja and Adanse, John Fynn who has worked on the Fante, and Irene Odotei who has worked for over a decade on the Ga and Dangme. Their collections are extremely rich sources of reference for archaeologists and linguists researching in these areas.

Fig. 1.7 Buipewura, Takurah I and state councillors narrating oral traditions of Buipe (October 1979)

Historical linguistics and linguistic dating

In the task of reconstructing the past, archaeology has an ally in linguistics. Languages all over the world are constantly undergoing changes in their different parts, their grammar, semantics, phonology and morphology. Such is this process of change that different groups of people speaking the same language may after some time lose contact and begin to speak different dialects or forms of the language. Later, the accumulated change may render some of the dialects so different as to make them separate languages. The task of the linguistic scholar is to identify the related languages of an area and to determine the extent to which they are related and the extent to which they have diverged from each other. Languages comprise traditionally-inherited vocabulary as well as vocabulary borrowed from other languages with which they have had contact in the past. In general, the scholar of historical linguistics seeks to compare words either (a) as a means of elucidating the internal history of the languages and the development of their sound systems and morphologies, or (b) for the purpose of studying the vocabulary itself to discover what has been inherited and what has been borrowed. For instance, the study of the cultural and economy-related words used in extant languages can help trace the ideas and objects diffused among them in antiquity.

The survival in a language of place-names makes it possible to identify ancient sites. Toponymy, or the study of place-names, provides clues to the identity of the historical founders of towns or to the nature of their location, their environment or their function in antiquity. Linguists distinguish what is known as a 'proto-language', that is the parent language spoken before changes occurred in the speech of the groups of people speaking it and so produced different languages. Thus Latin is more or less the proto-language of Spanish, French, Italian, etc. Similarly, the term 'Volta-Comoe' has been invented by scholars in Ghana to describe an ancient language now represented by all the languages of the 'Volta-Comoe' group including Akan, Guan and Bia. It is possible for language scholars to postulate a proto-language, delimit the probable area in which it was spoken and elucidate various aspects of the culture of the speakers of the languages. Such data can be correlated with archaeological evidence related to a culture having approximately the same characteristics. Through linguistic studies, it is possible to work out a relative chronology of language development and associated historical developments.

In the 1950s, a linguist, Morris Swadesh, impressed by the efficiency of radiocarbon dating, devised an absolute dating method for linguistics called glotto-chronological lexicostatistics. This scheme is based on a number of assumptions: firstly, that in a language, a basic core of non-cultural vocabulary (including terms for numerals, pronouns, geographical features, etc.) is less subject to change than other parts of the language; secondly, that the retention of words in the basic core of relatively stable vocabulary is constant through time. This means that given a certain number of basic words in a language, a certain percentage of these words will remain in the language after a thousand years

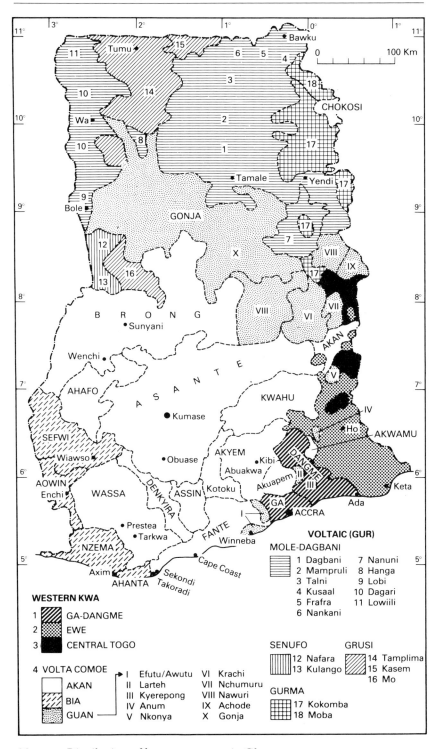

Map 1.1 Distribution of language groups in Ghana

and also after the passage of a third period of a thousand years, etc; thirdly, that the rate of loss of vocabulary is approximately the same in all languages. On the basis of these premises, Swadesh devised what he regarded as a universal formula for computing time elapsed since two or more genetically-related languages (derived from the same proto-language) ceased to be mutually intelligible or ceased to be dialects of a parent language. Although dates obtained in this way for most European languages accorded well with known historical facts, glotto-chonological dates obtained for some other languages have not agreed with the dates of documentary history.

The last two decades have witnessed the application of the canons of linguistic research in piecing together the story of the origins of different Ghanaian ethnic groups and their movements into, or within, Ghana. It has helped to postulate proto-languages and to ascertain the nature of languages which have diverged from the proto-languages and how changes in language and other aspects of culture reflect the general trend of cultural history. As a result of these studies and the genetic classification of languages into groups and sub-groups and dialects through comparative study of selected vocabulary, we now have a linguistic map of Ghana (Map 1.1). The study of place-names has aided archaeologists in the location of old sites. For instance, names such as Ahenkro (in the Volta basin) meaning royal town, Twifo Hemang (in central Ghana) meaning the royal seat of the Twi group of Ghana, are indicative of the political function of these sites. Among the Dangme one meaning of the word *doku* is deserted or derelict. When it is used to name a person it means a widow. But when it is attached as a suffix to the name of an ethnic group, it refers to a deserted township of the group. Thus the toponymy of Ladoku, Osudoku and Wodoku has enabled archaeologists to locate and study these old Dangme towns located in the hinterland of Accra.

Interesting linguistic research by Colin Painter and others on the Guan language group indicates that it is one of Ghana's most archaic group of languages. Probably the most extensive linguistic studies are those conducted on the Akan. These have demonstrated significant interaction of Akan peoples in an east-to-west direction between the Comoe and the lower Volta, and a north to south direction between the Volta confluence and the Atlantic coast. Several Akan dialects which have degrees of mutual intelligibility have been identified, namely, Akwapem, Akyem, Asante, Brong, Fante, and Wassa. Comparative field studies carried out by the linguist, Florence Dolphyne, have shown that the northern Akan of Brong have several conservative dialects, some of whose words and word structure are more archaic than those of the middle and southern Akan. The archaeology of the Brong region argues much older village and urban settlements than in middle and southern Akan. This has significant implications in the current debate on the origins and spread of the Akan. Oral traditions of the Brong and Takyiman, which are paralleled in Fanteland, state that some of the Fante migrated from the Takyiman area under their leaders, Obonomankoma, Oson, and Odapagyan. The effect of this migration is reflected in the close resemblance of Fante and Takyiman-Brong vocabulary related to their politico-social systems. One of the earliest linguistic studies carried out in Ghana was by the Dutchman, Pieter de Marees, who visited the country in 1601. De Marees made a cursory study of the Akan language spoken at Elmina in 1601 and published over three hundred words, many phrases and some dialogues in his book *Beschryvinge ende historiche verhael vaut gout Koninckrijck van Guinea*. Although De Marees's vocabulary list shows that the language spoken at Elmina at the time was Fante Akan, some of the words sound more archaic than their present-day Fante equivalents. It would appear that Elmina Fante was influenced by Adanse and Assin to the north of the Elmina coast, probably through the gold trade linking Fanteland with Mali through Adanse area.

Another linguist, Kropp Dakubu, has made a detailed study of Ga and Dangme languages. It is clear from her research that Ga and Dangme are closely related and that the two languages diverged from a common proto-Ga-Dangme ancestral language. Modern Ga and Dangme are mutually unintelligible although large numbers of Dangme speakers learn Ga. They have more vocabulary and grammatical dis-similarities than similarities. A study of cultural vocabulary shows that both languages have been heavily influenced by surrounding languages with which they have been in contact through the commercial, cultural, and migrational activities of their speakers. Ga and Dangme have each borrowed a small percentage of vocabulary, especially that related to economic activities and statecraft, from Guan of the Accra and Akwapem area and from Akan of the Akwapem, Asante, and Akyem areas. Ga seems to have lost more indigenous words of proto-Ga-Dangme and borrowed more material from outside. Dangme has tended to stick more to its indigenous vocabulary. On the other hand, recent studies have shown that certain changes occurred in Dangme first, and only later spread to Ga. The linguistic evidence is confirmed by archaeology. Dangme pottery manufactured in Shai between A.D. 1300 and 1750 is found on sites of the Ga and Dangme of that period, and Dangme pottery of A.D. 1600 and 1750 is found on Guan and Akan sites in Akwapem.

During field studies on Ga-Dangme oral traditions and historical linguistics, the author collected information which suggests that proto-Ga-Dangme speakers probably had a subsistence economy based on millet (*nmaa*) and yam (*hie/yele*) cultivation. The same word (*nmaa*) is used to mean both corn (millet) and food. This archaic word where it refers to food has been replaced by the modern word *niyeni*. Also, millet is grown by the modern Ga only for serving food to the traditional gods during the annual Ga *homowo* (meaning, 'hooting at hunger') festival held in commemoration of the deliverance of the Ga by their gods from severe famine of pre-European times. After the introduction of maize by the early Europeans, *abele* (maize) was adopted as the general word for corn. Archaeological excavations in the old settlement sites of the Ga-Dangme have revealed only querns and mullers (Fig. 1.3), probably used for the preparation of unknown types of food since any remains of corn, etc., would long have disappeared from the ground. It is in such cases that historical linguistics can provide an aid to archaeology. The cultivation of millet by the earliest ancestors of the Ga, said by local custodians of oral history at Ayawaso to have come from savanna country north or north east of the Accra plains, raises the question of the place of origin of the Ga-Dangme, especially since there are no wild prototypes of millet growing now in the Accra plains.

It has been suggested that the relatively wide distribution of Akan and the high incidence of mutual intelligibility among its dialects indicates a more recent spread than Ga and Dangme. From a glotto-chronological analysis of languages of southern Ghana, Colin Painter has suggested that the Volta-Comoe group of languages probably began to diverge from Ewe and Ga-Dangme sometime in the mid-second millennium B.C., that the Tano and Guan sub-groups of Volta-Comoe languages became differentiated around the first half of the first millennium B.C., and that Ga and Dangme probably separated from their parent language sometime around the eighth century A.D.

2   The search for Ghana's past

The first people to interest themselves in the Ghanaian past and in archaeological objects or cultural materials were the ancient Ghanaians themselves.

Prehistoric studies show that in many parts of the world, even before systematic archaeology began, local people discovered what they thought to be ancestral man-made artifacts on the ground and that they speculated on their origins and uses, though they tended to attach a supernatural significance to them. It has not been otherwise in Ghana. Ghanaians of the last three centuries, whether they found polished stone axes or 'aggrey beads' or biconically-perforated stones, naturally exposed after a rainstorm, attributed them either to the supernatural or to their ancestors.

Winwood Reade, who visited Ghana, then called the Gold Coast, in the 1870s and was a correspondent for *The Times* during the 1874 British–Asante war, wrote in *The Story of the Ashante Campaign:*

> One morning, Mr. Zimmermann of the Basel Mission at Odumasi, near the Volta brought me a stone which had evidently been shaped by human hands into the image of an axe. With these tools the ancestors of the white men, the red men, and the black men, had hewed down the oaks of Europe, the cedars of Asia, the pines of America, and the huge silk cotton trees of Negroland. Not only are these stone implements dug up all over the world, but they are supposed by the common people to be thunderbolts. As regards Western Africa, this belief is easily explained. After heavy storms of rain, which are usually accompanied by thunder and lightning the upper soil is washed away, the stone implements are found lying on the ground, and so seem to have fallen from the sky.

In Ghana not all those who interested themselves in these objects believed that they had a celestial origin. Rattray, in his book *Ashanti* (1923), documented oral traditions concerning the origin of polished axes: 'The so-called "God's axes"', Rattray wrote,

> were really tools used by the ancestors in the past, not only previously to, but contemporaneously with, a period when the smelting of iron was practised. Kakari, an exceptionally intelligent Ashanti, gave me the following statement before I was aware of the existence of the very long celts: 'My grandfather, Kakari Panyin, once told me that he had been told by his grandfather who himself had heard of, but had not seen them in use, that very long ago, the

Ashanti used the stone hoes which are now called "Nyame Akuma". These axes were not originally the short things now found but were very long, and that they used them for hoeing, holding them in both their hands and digging between their open legs . . . . Later, and after I had seen the long celts, another old man, Kobina Wusu, told me that very long ago the Ashanti used hoes made of stone a cubic long, demonstrating this by holding out the right arm, fingers pointing, and touching the elbow-joint with the left hand'.

(Rattray, 1923, p. 323)

Thus Ghanaians of the period of Karikari, Kakari Panyin, and Kobina Wusu, and their immediate ancestors, that is about A.D. 1600–1900, showed that they were not unaware of the historical and technological nature of artifacts now known to be of an archaeological character. But the first people to apply archaeological methodology to these material remains and use them as a historical source were the European visitors to Ghana.

One of the earliest recorded references to prehistoric study in Ghana is that of the Danish missionary, Monrad. In 1822 Monrad described ground stone axes which he had found on Stone Age settlement sites at Osu, Accra. These tools were taken for study to the Danish Royal Ethnographic Museum in Copenhagen which was at the time known to be 'unrivalled in the world for its relics of the age of stone'. Some were also deposited in the Dutch Royal Museum of Antiquities at Leyden. This was precisely the time when the Danish pioneers of European archaeology, Christian Thomsen and J. J. Worssae, curators of the Danish National Museum, were discussing the 'Three Age System', the idea that all the vast array of scattered and hitherto incoherent ancient materials could be classified on the basis of a technological model in the chronological succession, Stone Age, Copper or Bronze Age, and Iron Age.

Before Monrad's publication, the interest of European visitors to Ghana had been aroused by what was known as the 'aggrey bead' whose origin and mode of manufacture both puzzled and intrigued them. In the early 16th century, Pereira had speculated about it and described it as 'a blue cory bead'. Barbot wrote in the 1680s about 'blue stones called agory or acorry'. Bowdich wrote in 1819 that 'the natives invariably declare that the aggrey beads are found in the Dankara, Akim, Warsaw, Ahanta, and Fantee countries . . . they say they are directed to dig for them by a spiral vapour issuing from the ground and that they rarely lay near the surface, the finder is said to be sure of a series of good fortune'. Of course, this pursuit was for the locals probably more in the line of treasure-hunting than historical scholarship, a feature of Egyptian and Near Eastern antiquarianism in the 19th and early 20th centuries. Nevertheless, it is interesting that even at such an early date, this topic which is today still a subject of debate and controversy attracted local and foreign interest. Winwood Reade, once his curiosity had been aroused, looked for more sites and succeeded in finding polished stone axes in a number of sites in Akwapim and Asante. Reade's discoveries, the first West African stone tools to reach England, were exhibited at the British Anthropological Association's Liverpool meeting in 1870 and were also put on exhibition by the London Ethnological Society. His finds served as comparative material in discussions on prehistoric terminology among British archaeological scholars of the day and were the subject of an illustrated paper written by Sir John Lubbock (later Lord Avebury), a pioneer of British archaeology who introduced into archaeology the terms 'Palaeolithic' (Old Stone Age) and 'Neolithic' (New Stone Age). Meanwhile the circle of enthusiasts on Ghana's past widened. One of them, Burton, recalled his experiences:

> I nailed to the wall of our sitting room (at Axim) a rough print showing the faces and profiles of stone implements (of the neolithic or ground type) and drew to it the attention of all native visitors. The result was that the people began bringing specimens at once. The supply continued to come in, both up and down the coast, until I had secured thirteen fragments and entire specimens. When, however, the vendors found that value was attached to their wares, the price rose from a shilling to a dollar, and at least £100 was freely talked of.
> (*Journal of the Anthropological Institute*, 12, 1883, p. 450)

In the early years of this century, officials of the colonial administration stepped up the process of archaeological surface collection. Kitson, the Director of the Geological Survey, reported in 1916 at the end of a three-year country-wide study tour that he had found several thousands of quartz and quartzite 'palaeolithic' and 'neolithic' tools in different parts of the country. His finds led him to write in the *Geological Journal of the Gold Coast* (1916): 'There is evidence throughout the country of its occupation by people who lived there before the present peoples came into the lands.' Kitson collected from Kintampo district, Jemaa,

Fig. 2.1 Stone palette, previously named 'terracotta cigar' or 'rasp'

Busunu, Tulundo, and Buipe district in Northern Ghana and Northern Asante many examples of what he described as 'round-ended, flattened pieces of weathered clay stone or burnt clay, which are either plain or are ornamented with longitudinal, transverse, and oblique cuts, making check patterns of various kinds (Fig. 2.1). These artifacts are examples of the well-known Kintampo culture objects to be discussed later in chapter five.

Kitson noted that the local people had no idea what these objects were used for but that 'they regard them as of similar origin to the stone implements'. This recognition, on the part of non-literate local people, of an association between the polished stone axe and the 'round-ended flattened pieces of clay stone', an association which has been proved in several scientific excavations, is quite clearly good 'archaeological observation'. Kitson also described grinding hollows and grooves along the banks of the Volta river which he attributed to the Ghanaian aboriginals.

N. R. Junner, Kitson's successor as Director of the Geological Survey, widened the scope of his department's archaeological activities and undertook studies on ancient pottery collections, iron-smelting sites and stone circles. In the early 1930s, Junner carried out reconnaissance surveys of ancient entrenchments and mounds located in Akyem Kotoku and Akwapem. In 1934, he proceeded to carry out the first archaeological excavation of some of the earthworks at Abodum in Akyem. He noted the stratification of stone axes associated with pottery in the upper levels above a level containing remains of iron furnace structures and iron slag, the waste product of iron-smelting. He also made a bold attempt at classifying the pottery finds. Junner showed insight into the research strategies most suitable for traditional societies by initiating the correlation of oral traditions and excavated data. From his consultations with the traditional historians of Akyem Kotoku, he reported that the local inhabitants disclaimed any knowledge of the origin or purpose of the trenches but added that they pre-dated the arrival of their ancestors in Akyem Kotoku.

H. J. Braunholtz of the British Museum, London, who paid an official visit to West Africa in 1936 and quickly familiarized himself with the available data on Ghanaian archaeology, observed in a report which was published in *Antiquity* in 1936:

> The building of roads and railways, mining and dredging operations and agriculture have at various times produced, as by-products, a considerable amount of archaeological materials in the Gold Coast. Large unpublished collections made by the Directors of the Geological Survey are deposited at the survey's offices in London and Accra. These activities have shown the existence of stone age cultures of both palaeolithic and neolithic facies, the latter characterized by distinctive faceted celts and apparently overlapping the local Iron Age without the intervention of copper or bronze . . . . A new chapter in the archaeological history of the colony was opened in 1931 by Dr. N. R. Junner . . . when he found and surveyed certain ancient trenches between Manso and Akwatia.

Braunholtz's plea for more publication received a fitting answer from Captain R. P. Wild, Inspector of Mines, and an archaeological enthusiast. He published a number of papers in local and overseas journals on a variety of ethnographic and archaeological topics, including polished stone axes, Stone Age pottery, Akan terracotta sculptures, bead-making, and iron-smelting. His archaeological publications were based on a careful study of artifacts excavated from the mines and they provided useful resource material for later scholars. By making use of the *Gold Coast Review* and the *Gold Coast Teachers' Journal* he initiated a programme of popularising archaeology, at least among the educated class in Ghana.

In 1937, Thurstan Shaw, an archaeologist, was appointed curator of the Achimota College Museum of Anthropology. With him began a new era of scientific excavation in Ghana. His excavation in 1940 of the Late Stone Age site of Bosumpra cave at Abetifi, Kwahu, was the first of its kind on a Ghanaian Stone Age site. It produced thousands of quartz microliths, polished stone axes, stone rubbers and pottery, all of which Shaw attempted to classify with great care. In a publication of 1932, Junner had described a large Iron Age mound, located at Dawu Asaman in Adukrom, Akwapem, which contained pottery, bones, as well as a gold bead at the bottom of the deposit. This caught the attention of Shaw. In 1942, he proceeded to excavate the Dawu mound with the help of students of Achimota College. The excavations unearthed over half-a-million potsherds, smoking pipes, clay sculptures, brass-casting moulds and crucibles, copper and iron implements, molluscs, beads, and cowrie shells.

In 1961, Shaw published a full report entitled *Excavation at Dawu*. In it, he provided a detailed analysis of the excavation and the finds. He also made a scholarly attempt at answering some of the crucial questions about Iron Age Ghana. It is clear from his book that he had interviewed local people and recorded oral traditions in the hope that some of the traditions would shed light on the makers of the mound, on the cultural contents, and their date. He had little success in obtaining a definite answer as to whether the site was a Guan or an Akan site. He had even less luck in his attempt to solve, once and for all, the problem of the origin of the enigmatic 'aggrey bead'. But his discussion of the evidence of *cire-perdue* or lost-wax method of brass casting, his debate as to whether the practice of smoking tobacco and the local manufacture of smoking pipes was a result of European contact, and his pioneering use of the pipe as a guide-fossil for dating, all proved useful to the development of Ghanaian archaeology in the 1960s and 70s. The Dawu mound illustrates the Iron Age transition period just before and after the arrival of the Europeans along the coast.

One of the notable pioneers of Ghanaian archaeology was Richard Nunoo, who was a museum assistant at the Achimota Museum and who participated in Shaw's excavations at the Bosumpra cave, the Dawu mound and an iron-smelting site at Achimota College farm. In the course of his museum duties, Nunoo carried out ethnographic studies and reconnaissance surveys of archaeological sites and monuments such as the European coastal forts and castles and old Islamic mosques in northern Ghana. During the 1940s and 50s, Nunoo undertook excavations on Iron Age sites at Nsuta, Asebu, Beifikrom, Ayawaso, Akwamufie, the University drama studio site at Accra, and a Kintampo culture site at Kumasi University campus. His excavations at the drama studio site, Ayawaso, and Asebu, threw light on the processes of technological, commercial, and urban development among the Ga, Dangme, and Fante peoples of the period between the 14th and the 17th centuries.

In 1951, the national museum was set up in the newly-established Department of Archaeology at the University College of the Gold Coast, Achimota, under the headship of Professor A. W. Lawrence. Lawrence's detailed and well-illustrated book on the European forts and castles written during his term of office is a valuable contribution to the knowledge of early European architecture in Ghana and the economic and social functions associated with it.

When Ghana attained independence in 1957, most of the collections of the Legon museum of archaeology and anthropology was transferred to the new national museum built in the centre of Accra. H. D. Collings was appointed museum director and Nunoo became assistant curator. Nunoo provided the much-needed continuity for the museum from its inception and eventually rose to become its director, a post he still holds today.

In 1963, the Department of Archaeology at Legon, under the headship of Professor Peter Shinnie, initiated lecturing in archaeology to history undergraduates and also commenced a post-graduate degree course in African archaeology which gave a stimulus to archaeology.

Meanwhile, Oliver Davies had been appointed Reader in the Department of Archaeology. Davies believed that before archaeology could forge ahead with archaeological excavation and teaching on any substantial scale, it was of paramount importance that a general archaeological reconnaissance should be undertaken throughout the country and as many sites as possible mapped. Historians of Ghanaian archaeology will forever doff their hats to Davies. He spent ten months out of every year in the field, travelled thousands of kilometres through every part of Ghana. Where his Land-Rover could not reach, he did not hesitate to walk to carry out ground surveying. Between 1952 and 1966, he mapped over two thousand archaeological sites of differing periods ranging from Early Stone Age times to the nineteenth century A.D. He carried out ethnographic studies on contemporary traditional crafts. He ventured into the remotest areas to examine ancient goldmining pits. He was amazing in his capacity to combine detailed study with broad overall surveys. Davies excavated a unique Kintampo culture site at Ntereso. This site yielded elegant bone harpoons, stone arrowheads and evidence of early pastoralism dated by radiocarbon to the early second millennium B.C. In spite of his extensive reconnaissance work, he undertook thirteen other excavations, including the Stone Age sites of Limbisi, New Todzi, Legon Botanical Garden, Christian's Village, the Akan mausoleum site of Ahinsan which has shed so brilliant a light on the 17th-century burial sites, social custom, religion and philosophy of the early Akan, and also an entrenchment site at Kokobin which was a follow-up of Junner's work.

Davies's work on Stone Age chronology, tool identification, and especially his interpretations, have been criticised by several archaeologists as being inaccurate. Nevertheless, Ghana archaeology owes to him the great body of knowledge of archaeological sites which it now has in the series of four detailed monographs containing field notes which have been cyclostyled and circulated to learned institutions and museums in many parts of the world. In 1961, he published a monograph summing up archaeological knowledge on Ghana. He followed this up with two books on the prehistory of West Africa and several detailed mimeographed site-reports on his excavations at Ntereso, Ahinsan, and Mampongtin. He capped his achievements on Ghanaian archaeology with a survey of some 450 sites in the Volta basin between 1963 and 1966, when the Government of Ghana funded a salvage scheme in archaeology prior to the flooding of the Volta basin due to the construction of the Akosombo Dam. Davies co-ordinated the Volta Basin Research Project (V.B.R.P.) based at the University of Ghana which ran the multi-disciplinary salvage research. He was also, jointly with Peter Shinnie, the field supervisor of two research fellows, Richard York and Duncan Mathewson, who carried out excavations of some 23 sites which have provided Ghana with a substantial fund of knowledge on its past from Kintampo culture times to the 19th century. Among the sites excavated by this trio of Davies, York and Mathewson were Chukoto, a Kintampo culture site in the north, Kitare, a great earthwork site also in northern Ghana, New Buipe, the capital site of Old Gonja, Jakpawuase, the Palace of Jakpa (legendary founder of Gonja), and Akroso Beposo, a Later Iron Age trading site on the Volta.

With the commencement of small-scale university teaching in archaeology, Paul Ozanne was appointed lecturer in archaeology. To promote his teaching, Ozanne embarked on a detailed field study of the prehistory and the early history of the Ga-Dangme and the Akan in the area within fifty kilometres of Accra. He surveyed Late Stone Age sites, Kintampo culture sites, and Iron Age sites. He carried out trial excavations, among others, at Ayaso, capital of Great Accra, at Ladoku, early capital town of the Dangme people and at Nyanaoase, capital site of Akwamu. His legacy to Ghanaian archaeologists was the smoking pipe chronological sequence which he evolved for dating sites on coastal Ghana. He demonstrated from his excavations that the introduction of tobacco and imported pipes into the Ghanaian littoral stimulated the development of a local smoking pipe industry, and that the pipes not only betrayed cultural traits in their decorative styles, but also that their shapes followed a set pattern and changed with the passage of time. Using his pipe series, Ozanne was able to date sites whose Iron Age levels contained types of local pipe which had been found elsewhere at excavated sites of Ayaso and Ladoku associated with dated European imported pottery and European pipes, and, by extension, it was possible also to give relative dates to pre-pipe cultural levels. Ozanne's pipe sequence was, strictly speaking, worked out for the Accra plains whence he extended it to the Fante and Winneba coastlands. He later studied pipe styles in northern Ghana from one site. Subsequently, there has been a tendency to apply his sequence to inland sites which may well have followed a slightly different trend of development. Thus, although it can be said that local smoking pipes wherever they are found in Ghana date their sites to the post-1600 A.D. period, more care is needed in closer dating.

In 1968, a new epoch opened in Ghanaian archaeology with the introduction of an honours degree course at the University of Ghana. The Department of Archaeology became transformed from being an essentially research-oriented unit engaged in minor undergraduate and post-graduate teaching to a full-scale teaching department. The task of providing practical lessons on a regular basis necessitated the building of an archaeological field centre at Hani, in north-western Brong Ahafo, the site of Begho township, well-known from European and Arabic written records for its trade and cultural links with the Middle Niger region in antiquity. The idea of a semi-permanent field centre at Begho was conceived by Merrick Posnansky who took up the chair of archaeology at Legon in 1967. Thanks to financial support from the Leverhulme Trust and the University of Ghana, Posnansky was able to initiate the West African Trade Project (W.A.T.P.). Hitherto, excavations in Ghana had largely taken the form of short test-excavations which produced relatively small quantities of finds. The site of Begho has numerous mounds spread over an area of some eight kilometres square. This was an ideal site for carrying out a long-range area excavation that would elucidate the political, social, and economic life-style of this ancient Akan trading township.

Moreover, Begho's successor states in the Hani-Nsawkaw area have a rich legacy of oral traditions and traditional crafts. In Begho, Posnansky saw an excellent opportunity for trying a new inter-disciplinary approach to Ghanaian and West African archaeology. Linguists from Legon carried out a study of the multilingual structure of the successor populations of Old Begho, which involved research among people of the Mande, Gur, and Kwa-speaking language family groups. Ethno-botanists with interests in farming and collecting of wild crops, experts on ancient weights and measures, specialists in oral traditions and in various crafts such as pottery, cloth, metal work and traditional building came to join in the inter-disciplinary quest for the riches of Begho's past.

Altogether, some twenty-seven sites were excavated under the project between 1970 and 1979. The sites in the Hani area included two Kintampo culture sites which though not directly related to trade were nevertheless excavated to investigate the possibilities of early food production as a factor which prepared the way for urbanization at Begho. A total of twelve Iron Age sites were excavated at Begho. Funds of the project were also made available to University graduate students for research at the Brong sites of Bono Manso and Old Wenchi, and for excavations on prehistoric sites in Kwahu. In addition, a 17th-century Dutch fort site called Ruychaver, located on the river Ankobra, was excavated. Also, special experiments were carried out to ascertain the nature and rate of decay of traditional forms of architecture and the nature and rate of growth of rubbish dumps. These experiments were designed to extract information that would help the archaeologist who deals with sites where ancient house walls and other materials decay rapidly. Begho and the West African Trade Project illustrate how the wind of change which had been blowing for a decade over western archaeology, introducing the 'new archaeology' into Europe, America, and the Near East, had begun to be felt in West Africa and Ghana. But even before the w.a.t.p. was launched, the 'new archaeology' had begun its leavening influence in 'neolithic' studies in Ghana. In 1966 and 1967, Colin Flight, a lecturer in archaeology at Legon employed the flotation analysis which had been applied in neolithic studies in Europe and the Near East in his excavations at Kintampo rockshelter. This analysis provided the first indications that oil palm and cow peas had a place in the subsistence economy of the Kintampo 'neolithic' culture of Ghana. In 1974, Francis Musonda excavated two rockshelters in Kwahu and used the flotation method to recover specimens of oil palm found in association with microliths, pottery and stone beads.

One crucial factor in the development of archaeology in Ghana, as has already been pointed out in chapter 1, has been the introduction of the use of radiocarbon dating. In assessing the role of radiocarbon dating in the history of archaeology, Dr. Glyn Daniel observed in his book, *The Origins and Growth of Archaeology* (1967), 'it could be said that with the arrival of an absolute chronology through radiocarbon dating archaeology may be said to be fully grown'. Debatable though the wording of Daniel's view on radiocarbon dating may be, it nevertheless contains a gem of truth.

The v.b.r.p. excavations produced twenty-one radiocarbon dates while the w.a.t.p. produced twenty-five dates. The impact of radiocarbon dating on Ghanaian archaeology was so vivifying that it became necessary for some sites excavated within the last thirty years to be re-excavated in order to place them in the chronology of Ghanaian prehistory and early history. The Bosumpra cave, excavated by Shaw in 1940, was re-excavated with the result that one of the lowest levels with microliths produced evidence suggesting that local pottery-making in Ghana may date back to the middle of the fourth millennium B.C. More dates will be required to confirm this evidence. The Akyem Kotoku earthworks which Junner and Davies had excavated previously were re-excavated by Kiyaga-Mulindwa, who obtained radiocarbon dates around the middle of the 15th century A.D. for the Atwea cultural level overlying the earthworks, thus suggesting a pre-European date for them.

More recently, the author initiated the Accra plains archaeological and historical project aimed at carrying out an inter-disciplinary study into the early technology, economy and culture of the peoples of the Accra plains. This has necessitated a fresh look at the early towns of Ladoku and Ayawaso excavated by Paul Ozanne in the 1960s. Radiocarbon dates obtained from excavations at Ladoku in 1977–79 indicate that urbanization began in Dangmeland by the 14th century A.D., and that in the 16th century the township of La developed to become the prosperous capital of the Dangme, involved in trade with the Europeans along the coast.

3 The land, its people and culture

A country's past is best studied and interpreted against the background of its environment. Indeed, it is the interplay of such features as geology, relief, drainage, climate, vegetation and fauna and man's reaction to it that dictates the patterns of population, agricultural, industrial, and cultural development.

Ghana holds a relatively central position in West Africa. Sandwiched between Ivory Coast, Togo and Upper Volta, its northern border looks towards the Sahel, Sudan, and Sahara while its southern coastline borders the Atlantic Ocean. This location has very much influenced the trend of Ghana's development both in the past and in more recent times.

Relief and drainage

Most of Ghana consists of lowland not exceeding 350 metres above sea level. Mount Afadjato, the highest point in the country is less than 1 000 metres above sea level. Yet the relief structure shows some contrasting features. The forest zone, in particular, displays considerable variety in relief. For, although most of the forest land is made up of peneplains, there are uplands here and there, such as the Akwapem ranges which rise from below 100 metres near the coast to around 350 metres in the northwest. The forest zone is also marked in some places by quite steep gradients between valleys and hilltops thanks to erosion along the channels of streams under forest vegetation. On the other hand, gentler undulations occasioned by greater surface erosion under savanna vegetation characterise the savanna country. Steep slopes in the savanna areas take the form of inselbergs which are prominent in southeast and northwest Ghana. One of the most striking features of Ghana's relief structure is the Voltaian scarp which extends over an area of nearly 200 kilometres across middle Ghana and is outstanding in the Gambaga area.

Ghana is drained by a number of rivers. The Volta and its tributaries which easily dominate the drainage system cover over 65 per cent of the country. Smaller rivers such as the Ankobra, Ayensu, Birim, Densu, Ofin, Pra, and Tano drain into the sea. Ghana's only sizeable natural lake, Bosumtwi, is believed to have been formed some $1\frac{1}{2}$ million years ago by the impact of a large meteorite from outer space.

Climate and vegetation

Ghana's location between latitudes $4°44'$ and $11°11'$ North accounts for its tropical equatorial climate. Temperatures are quite high, ranging between 77.9°F (25.5°C) and 84.2°F (29°C). The climatic pattern is determined by the movements of two airstreams – the hot dry tropical continental air mass from the northeast and the moist cooler southwest monsoon from the Atlantic ocean. The distribution and timing of rainfall depends largely on the northward and southward movement of the intertropical convergence zone, the meeting point of the northeast and southwest winds. The principal features of rainfall in Ghana are its seasonal character and its variability from year to year. The average annual rainfall is greatest in the southwest corner of the country (86 inches or 2184mm.) but decreases northward and eastward reaching 60 inches (1524mm.) around Kumase, 30 inches (762mm.) in the Accra plains, and 42 inches (1066mm.) along the northern frontier. In southern Ghana, there are two rainy seasons from May to July and from September to November, while in the north there is only one main season from April to September. Another striking feature of the rainfall is the relative dryness of the Accra plains, a feature which has been attributed firstly to the moist monsoon current which blows parallel to the coastline, and secondly to an area of cold water east of Cape Three Points which cools the ocean and makes the monsoon current lose most of its moisture (Map 3.1)

The types of vegetation in Ghana are dictated by a number of factors such as climate, topography, and soil as well as the activities of living organisms including man. On the whole, however, it is climate, and especially the rainfall aspect of it, which determines the vegetation pattern and so influences the trend of agricultural and other human activities. Consequently, the regions receiving between 63 inches (1600mm.) and 53 inches (1346mm.) rainfall have high forest with large trees. The regions north of the forest and also the southeast coast which receive 39 to 59 inches have tree savanna. On the other hand, the area between Sekondi and the Accra plains west of the Volta receives only 32 to 35 inches (812–889mm.) and so is characterised by open grassland with isolated baobab trees (Map 3.2).

Geology

The geological map of Ghana depicts contrasting rock features, some formed around 3 000 million years ago while others were only formed between 400 and 500 million years ago.

Over half of Ghana is underlain by some of the country's oldest rocks, namely the pre-Cambrian sedimentary rocks which have undergone metamorphic and folding activities in the past. In the eastern part of Ghana, the pre-Cambrian rocks bear the name 'Dahomeyan' while those of the west are termed 'Birrimian'. Nearly all the rest of the country is within the Voltaian basin and the valleys of its tributaries. This basin is made up of Palaeozoic sandstone and shale sedimentary rocks formed during the last 500 to 300 million years ago. The Palaeozoic rock system which is underlain by 'Birrimian' rocks account for the continuous steep escarpment strikingly evident in the area between Koforidua and Wenchi and also in the Gambaga area.

In contrast to the interior regions of Ghana, the coastlands have a relatively younger sedimentary rock system ranging from the late

Palaeozoic to the early Cenozoic formed between 400 and 500 million years ago. The Accra plains, for instance, though underlain by extensive pre-Cambrian 'Dahomeyan' gneiss deposits have some of the most

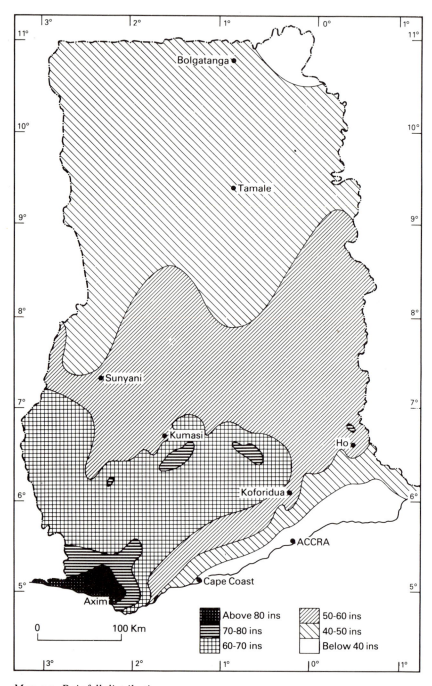

Map 3.1 Rainfall distribution

recent rocks formed between the Devonian and the Tertiary periods. The fossil of a marine anthropod called the trilobite dating to about 300 million years ago has been found in the Devonian shales of Accra beach

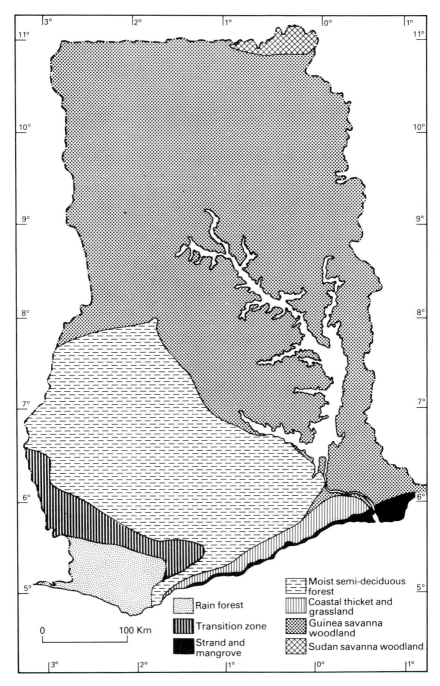

Map 3.2 Vegetation zones

and is now in the University geological museum at Legon. Similarly, relatively young Cenozoic rocks occur in the Volta delta region and in the areas of Axim and Sekondi. Between the Axim and Accra coast-lands, the interplay of Devonian sediments and pre-Cambrian rocks provides a beautiful scenic effect of alternating sandy beaches and headlands.

The quest for knowledge of Ghana's geology was pioneered in the early 19th century by scholars such as Thomas Park, son of the cele-brated explorer of the Niger, Dr. Stranger, Sir Charles Bullen, and later the officers of the Ghana Geological Survey established in 1913. The early geologists were actuated as much by academic as by more practical and utilitarian motives. The older rocks of Ghana are rich in econ-omically exploitable minerals including gold, diamonds, bauxite, and manganese. Gold is of particular interest to the archaeologist and historian since it was mined in pre-European times, probably as early as the 14th century and provided the basis for long-distance trade between the Akan, on the one hand, and the Mande and European traders on the other hand. Gold is known to occur in the contact zones between the 'Birrimian' metamorphic rock system and the 'Tarkwaian' folded range and also in the pre-Cambrian conglomerate horizons of the Tarkwaian rock system.

Ghana, though a relatively well-watered country, has over the ages faced the problem of how to conserve and use water. Rainfall water either sinks into the underlying sub-soil and rock or is transported by streams into the sea, or it simply evaporates. Whether or not this water can be conserved and used depends chiefly on the local geological features. The porous and permeable sandstone rocks of Ghana allow water to pass through them and penetrate the sub-soil and so the water is preserved and can be exploited through the boring of wells. Clayey and shale rocks do not allow water to pass through them and are most invaluable in their ability to trap water either on the surface or in

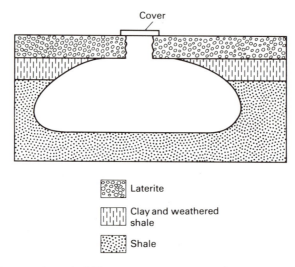

Fig. 3.1 Cross-section of a biliga

permeable rocks beneath. Crystalline rocks such as granites, metamorphic rocks and the Voltaian compacted and cemented rocks do not permit water passage through their pores and interstices but are nevertheless able to hold water in spaces separating joints, especially where there has been extensive weathering in the joints. In the past, and in present-day rural areas without pipe-borne water systems, rivers, surface springs and wells have been the main source of water supply for domestic consumption, agriculture and industry. Many archaeological sites in Ghana are located along or close to rivers and their tributaries and surface springs. As early as the middle of the second millennium B.C., some early pastoralist communities at Hani in northwest Brong Ahafo are known to have dug up fairly deep cisterns as a solution to the problem of scarcity of water. Excavation of some of these prehistoric cisterns has yielded domestic pottery and other cultural material of the period. This tradition of constructing cisterns was continued by the Iron Age people of Begho who were successors of the early pastoralist communities. Due to the impermeable sedimentary shale rocks of the central Voltaian basin around Atebubu, Salaga, Tamale and Nasia, surface springs are generally lacking in the area. Since flood waters which accumulate on the surface in the wet season soon afterwards evaporate, the only devise for storage of surface water in these areas is the *biliga*. The *biliga* (Fig. 3.1) is a rock cistern or water tank excavated from the shale. The storage capacity of a *biliga* may range from 500 gallons (2275 litres) to several thousand gallons. In Dagombaland, where the term *biliga* originated, there are examples still in use which traditions date to a few hundred years back. Derelict *biligas* have been recorded on archaeological sites in association with Gonja 'tower-houses', painted pottery and 15th-century Kisoto pottery. Without the *biligas* it is difficult to see how central Gonja could have sustained such a large population as is believed to have occupied the area between A.D. 1000 and 1700.

Soils

Soil is the surface part of the earth's crust which is formed as a result of the breaking up of rocks or minerals under the impact of local climate and drainage and the action of plant and animal remains. Soil is enriched by plant and animal remains and is, in its turn, able to provide nutrients for living plants and the myriad micro-organisms that vary from season to season. It is not without reason, therefore, that soil has been described as a sort of living organism.

Soils vary according to local geological, climatic and vegetational conditions. The different types of soil in Ghana have been classified and mapped on the bases of their different nutrient and moisture properties and their relative content of acids, alkalines, and chemicals.

In the forest, there are two main types of soil – the ochrosols and oxysols. The nutrient quality of the ochrosols is seriously affected when forest is completely cleared because of the high rainfall which causes oxidation and leaching. Traditional crop farmers have overcome this problem through careful maintenance of the top-soil by the use of two methods. These are: partial forest clearing which helps quick regeneration of vegetation; and mixed cropping of long-term crops such as cassava, cocoyam, or plantain with short-term crops such as cereals and legumes. Oil palm, cocoa, coffee, and kola thrive on the forest ochrosols but can only be produced on a commercial scale on upland soils. The forest oxysols which are concentrated in south-west Ghana and on the Tarkwaian and Lower Birrimian rocks are strongly affected by the higher incidence of rainfall and are thus suitable mainly for the production of oil palm, rice, and rubber.

The soils of the interior savanna zone have a very much lower content of organic matter and phosphate, while their subsoils contain an unfavourable iron pan, their top-soils are erodible and in many places the rainfall is less reliable than in the forest zone. Hence, the potential of soil productivity has, in the past, as in recent times, been much less in this zone than in the forest. The savanna ochrosols which are concentrated in areas with a single maximum rainfall of 40 to 55 inches (1016–1397mm.) are extensively farmed among the northern Akan of Brong Ahafo, northeast Asante, as well as the Volta region and around Tamale and Gambaga. The relatively deep savanna ochrosols of the Voltaian sandstones have long been the leading areas in Ghana for the production of yam, guinea corn and millet. On the other hand, the southern savanna ochrosols have been noted for the production of maize. In the coastal savanna zone of the Accra plains and the Ho-Keta plains, rainfall is relatively low and the savanna ochrosols there have been cultivated chiefly for the production of drought-resisting crops such as millet, maize, guinea corn, cassava and groundnuts in addition to pastoralism.

Agriculture

Agriculture is the linch-pin of Ghana's economy. It is estimated that the economic activities of 70 per cent of the working population in most parts of the country are connected with agricultural pursuit. In northern Ghana, this percentage is higher. Although in a few places in the country agriculture has assumed a mechanised character, the general trend is still that of traditional agriculture using the same tools (fire, the iron hoe, axe, cutlass and sickle) previously employed by Iron Age farmers. Subsistence farmers throughout the country practise interplanting of annual and perennial crops as a device for reducing the risk of total crop disaster and also for providing cover for the exposed soil. In hilly areas, terrace cultivation is used as an effective method of dealing with the problem of soil erosion on farms. For instance, in the Lawra district of northern Ghana, and on the gneiss inselbergs of Dangmeland in the Accra plains, there are extant old cultivation terraces in the form of retaining wallings which traditions attribute to ancestral farmers of the last three hundred years or so. Generally speaking, in the forest zone today, conditions favour the cultivation of cocoa on a plantation scale, yam, cocoyam, plantain, banana, maize, rice, cassava, vegetables and fruits. The coastal savannas are not so prolific and only a few areas with favoured soils such as near Ada, the Ho-Keta plains and the Akwapem–Togo foothills are suitable for even medium-scale agriculture. On the other hand, the interior savannas are prolific in cattle rearing and the production of yam and cereals, especially guinea corn, millet, rice, and groundnuts.

Several of the domesticated food plants now grown in the forest zone were probably originally introduced from the savanna, for example, the yellow yam (*Dioscorea cayenensis*), the white yam (*Dioscorea rotundata*) which have large tubers adapted for food storage during the dry season, and the oil palm (*Elaeis guineensis*), originally grown in the forest-savanna margins because of its dislike for deep shade. The African rice (*Oryza glaberrima*) is also probably a derivative of a savanna grass adapted to shallow holes that dry up in the dry season. One of the few exceptions to this general rule is kola (*Cola nitida*) which is indigenous to the forest zone. Its area of highest production is the belt in Asante which stretches from the Pra river to Techiman but it is also produced in the centre and north of the zone with average rainfall of 50 to 60 inches (1270–1524mm.) per year. As the kolatine drug contained in the nut has stimulating and sustaining qualities, kola, especially the red nut, is highly popular amongst Muslim populations inhabiting the regions of northern Ghana, northern Nigeria, Mali, Niger, Upper Volta, and northward to the Saharan region as well as Muslim populations inhabiting the forest regions of West Africa. In the past, Asante farmers are known to have head-loaded kola to trading posts in northern Asante where they met buyers from northern Ghana and Hausaland. Northern buyers also journeyed south with donkeys to buy nuts.

The oil palm is one of the indigenous crops which have played an important role in the subsistence and export economy of Ghana in the past. Although it has a wide distribution throughout Ghana, its areas of greatest concentration are Kroboland, the area embracing Winneba, Swedru, and Saltpond, Ahanta, and eastern Nzema. A few other tree crops, namely the shea butter (*Butyrospermum parkii*), the baobab (*Adansonia digitata*), the fan palm (*Borassus aethiopum*), the *dawadawa* (*Parkia clappertoniana*) have served the subsistence needs of Ghana's savanna-dwelling populations as much in past centuries as in recent times.

Of the root crops which are cultivated in Ghana, the yellow yam and the white yam are known to have an indigenous origin in the West African savanna. The botanist, Burkill, has observed of the yellow yam: 'to the African is entirely due its invention as a crop plant'. The *Dioscorea praehensilis*, which is indigenous to the forest, still grows wild in the forest of Ghana and is used today as a source of food in times of famine. The indigenous West African origin of a number of cereals now grown has been established, among them, the Guinea corn (*Sorghum vulgare*), some forms of pearl millet (*Pennisetum typhoides*), fonio (*Digitaria exilis*), iburu (*Digitaria iburua*), and West African rice (*Oryza glaberrima*). Similarly, the wild ancestor of the Bambara groundpea (*Voandzeia subterranea*) has been identified in Adamawa, Cameroons, indicating its West African origin.

It would appear, therefore, that most of the root and cereal crops listed above were probably among the vital subsistence crops cultivated in Ghana prior to the introduction of New World and Asiatic crops. From A.D. 1500 onwards, thanks to the opening of the maritime sea route, the relative isolation of Ghanaian and West African agriculture was ended. Indigenous crop-plants were carried in Portuguese ships to the New World and a number of them, such as the West African *Dioscorea* yams, were first studied and named in the New World. In return, there was an even greater introduction of crop-plants into Ghana and West Africa: from Asia came the water yam (*Dioscorea alata*), Chinese yam (*Dioscorea esculenta*), taro cocoyam (*Colocosia esculenta*), Asiatic rice (*Oryza sativa*), and sugar cane (*Succharum spp.*); from the New World came pineapple (*Ananas canosus*), groundnut (*Arachis hypogaea*), cassava (*Manihot utilissima*), tannia cocoyam (*Xanthosoma sagittifolium*), the hard-grained flint maize (*Zea may*) of the Caribbean and Central America, and the soft-grained flour maize of Brazil.

Except perhaps the dwarf goat and sheep and the guinea-fowl, the livestock of Ghana has largely an external origin. For instance, the short-horn cow is thought to be a descendant of a number of principal racial groups including the large-horned, short-horned, lyre-horned Zebu and the hamitic long-horned. Over the centuries, cattle have been transported along the historic trade routes linking the Middle Niger and Hausaland with Ghana, bringing in different races of cattle which have been crossed from time to time. Thus, whereas the short-horned is common in the areas of Keta, Tongu, Nzema, and the Volta basin west of Yeji, the lyre-horned Zebu introduced from Mali is common in northeast Ghana. Similarly, the Ghana dwarf sheep has a countrywide distribution but the Fulani long-legged sheep has a mainly northern distribution. The horse, an importation from northern Africa via the West African Sudan was an important element in the process of state formation in the northern kingdoms of Mamprussi, Gonja, and Dagomba. It was also employed as a ceremonial piece or regalia item at the northern Akan courts of Begho and Bono Manso during the half century after A.D. 1300.

Population

Ghana's population as given by the 1970 census was 9.10 million. Its annual growth rate is estimated at nearly 3 per cent. Current (1980) estimates indicate that the population figure is around the 10 million mark. Of this, the highest population densities are concentrated in the urban and the cocoa-producing areas of southern Ghana and in the extreme northeastern section where intensive compound farming is practised.

The principal ethnic groups are the Akan (45 per cent), the Mole Dagbani (16 per cent), the Ewe (13 per cent), and the Ga-Dangme (9 per cent). Ghana has a multiplicity of languages and dialects all of which fall into two main linguistic groups, namely, the Kwa group of southern and middle Ghana and the Gur group of northern Ghana (see Map 1.1). The Kwa embraces (i) Akan (Twi-Fante) and their related languages, Nzema, Ahanta, Sefwi, and Aowin; (ii) Guan; (iii) Ewe; (iv) Ga, and (v) Dangme. Various languages of the Mande group of Mali are spoken in frontier towns which in the past had commercial links with towns outside the present political boundaries of Ghana. The Ligbi and Dyula dialects spoken in towns and villages in Brong Ahafo and northern Ghana are a case in point.

Akan is the largest single language group in Ghana. It is spoken by nearly 5 million people as a first language while another 4 million speak it as a second language. It is a prestige language because of the wealth, social standing and political power of its principal speakers in the historic period A.D. 1500 to the present day. Hence, not only have other languages like Guan, Ga-Dangme and Ewe been considerably influenced by Akan, but more and more Ghanaians have been using it either deliberately or undeliberately as a local *lingua franca* after the English language. Akan has been shown to be part of a wider Volta-Comoe language sub-family which includes the Cama and Mbato speakers of the Potou lagoon area and the Anyi-Baule of the Ivory Coast. The distribution of these languages and Akan in a continuous area from the southeastern Ivory Coast to the Volta river in eastern Ghana has been interpreted as indicating that the region of the Comoe River and the Ebrie and Potou lagoons which is the centre of the Volta-Comoe language group was the nuclear settlement area of the Akan from where they split. Akan dialects have a high degree of mutual intelligibility and are spoken over a wide geographical area. This is taken to be indicative of relatively recent population diffusion in Akanland.

On the other hand Guan is thought to be an older language group. Guan oral traditions show that the Guan are 'more indigenous' to Ghana than the Akan, some of whom state clearly that when they came into their present habitation they met the Guan already in occupation. It is thought that the original distribution pattern of Guan probably took the form of a crescent stretching from Gonja in northern Ghana to Awutu in Akwapim.

Culture

The traditional technology, arts, crafts and socio-political ideas of the Ghanaian past still survive to some extent today in spite of five centuries of competition with European and other imported ideas and goods. In a country in which there has been relative continuity in cultural tradition for several centuries in the case of certain traits, and up to three and a half millennia for other traits, ethnographic study is indispensable to the archaeologist and the historian alike. R. Sayce put the matter succinctly in his book *Primitive Arts and Crafts* (1933): 'without ethnography, archaeology would be blind of one eye and very short-sighted of the other'. Potting, one of the world's, and indeed Ghana's oldest crafts still thrives in various parts of the country. The ancient methods of shaping by hand, using the coil, modelling, moulding and multi-piece techniques, the ancient methods of decoration by incision, stamping, impression, roulette, clay-slip, paint, and smoke-glazing, and the pristine open air or bonfire method of baking pottery are still the rule rather than the exception. Many traditional pottery industries have been forced to close down either through competition with other foreign counterparts or through an interruption in the technique handed down, or through population movements.

Ethnographic studies have been conducted in several parts of the country, for instance, at Pankronu and Tafo in Asante, at Bondakile, Krobo, and Longoro Nkwanta in Brong Ahafo, in Akwapim, among the

LoDagaa, Gonja, Choruba, and Dagomba in northern Ghana, in Fante-land, and at Weija, Ningo, and Shai in the Accra plains. At Doryumu and Kodiabe, which are Dangme towns in the Shai area near Accra, pottery-making is today practised by nearly every family. In 1968, it was estimated that the Shai potters were producing some half a million pots annually, and that 'the potters of Shai can sell every pot they make, usually without the trouble of taking them to the market' (Quarcoo and Johnson, *Baessler-Archiv*, 16, 1968). This is a tribute to the high quality of Shai pottery, a tradition which has been maintained for some 200 to 300 years. One missionary who visited Shai in 1853 was astonished at the way they made pots 'as beautifully round as if they were turned on a potter's wheel'. Another missionary was so carried away by what he saw that he inflated his impressions and spoke of 'big pottery villages in Shai, whose pots supply almost the whole Gold Coast'. Similarly, at bondakile town near the ancient trading town of Begho in western Brong Ahafo pottery-making is a house-to-house commercial enterprise. Pottery-making is learnt by most young girls. Bondakile supplies all the neigh-bouring villages and towns as far as Bondoukou in the Ivory Coast. The fact that pottery types identical to those of Bondakile have been found in the ancient mounds of Begho shows that the Bondakile traditions go back at least to the 17th century. Pottery-making was raised to a fine art when, with the establishment of the Asante confederation, the Asante kings centralized all Asante arts and crafts in the neighbourhood of the capital, Kumasi. Tafo became the pottery metropolis. Here some of the best-quality polymorphic pottery with complex motifs was pro-duced, such as the *abusua kuruwa* or clan pot and the *mogyemogye* cere-monial jaw-bone pot, a wine jar used for pouring libation on the Golden Stool.

Iron technology, though now largely in a state of decline due to the flooding of the country with European manufactured iron bars after A.D. 1600, still maintains a foothold, however precariously, in a number of Ghanaian towns and villages such as Wawasi, Bamparase and Fumisua in Asante and Akpafu in the Volta region. In northern Ghana, the industry is still sporadically practised in several centres, as a recent ethnographic survey at Lawra, Zanlerigu, Cherepon, Jefisi, Tiza, Chiana, Busie, Billaw, Zuarungu and Sinibaga has shown. The reports of 19th-century European visitors and geologists engaged in field studies in the early 20th century show that iron-working was even more vigorously practised in the north between 1800 and 1930. Ethnography now provides fairly adequate information on the nature of the industry as practised since its inception in Ghana some two millennia ago. It is known, for instance, that the use of shaft furnaces has been, and is still general and that while some communities in northern Ghana employ bellows for ventilation, others – as at Akpafu – make use of the natural draught of the area; and also that whereas the Akpafu metallurgists dig shafts into the hillside to acquire their iron raw materials, the iron-workers of northern Ghana, Adanse in Asante, and in Brong Ahafo use iron oxides found in laterite blocks collected on the surface. Today, it is not an uncommon sight to find in local Ghanaian markets locally-made cutlasses, hoes, guns, animal-traps and knives.

Brass-casting, which is not so ancient a craft as iron technology, also survives in a few places in Ghana, among them Kurofofurom, a suburb in Kumasi, at Bono Manso and especially in northern Ghana, where there has been a tradition of manufacturing of bracelets, pendants, armlets, anklets and rings depicting naturalistic figures. Till recent times, brass-casters in Brong Ahafo and Asante were particularly adept at melting down European imported brass rods or manillas and using the lost-wax technique for making out of them gold weights, brass caskets for storing gold dust and brass vessels for storing shea butter, gold dust boxes, gold dust spoons, and maskettes. Thousands of gold weights made in this way are now scattered in collections of private people, museums and ethnographic institutions all over the world. To save the craft from utter demise, both the faculty of fine arts at the Kumasi University of Science and Technology and the Kumasi Arts Centre have institutionalised it while keeping its traditional character intact.

Ghana has a long tradition of gold-mining technology and gold smithing. Although today traditional gold-mining has totally ground to a halt (except the odd illegal practice of it), goldsmithery is still practised in some towns and villages. As early as 1471, the Portuguese, Pedro de Escobar, recorded the production of gold by local Ghanaians; and Jean Barbot noted that in 1622 the King of Guaffo was promoting gold-mining near Little Kommenda. Local Ghanaians were without doubt mining gold before the advent of Europeans.

Gold was obtained in the past by the locals mainly from alluvial and superficial deposits which were either of the residual type produced by rock-weathering *in situ*, or of the stream placer type. Stream placers were exploited by direct panning, that is by swirling the deposits from the stream bed around in stream water in large shallow pans so that the lighter dirt was washed away while the heavier gold stayed in the bottom of the pan. Residual placers were exploited by first digging a shaft down to the deposit, removing the pay-dirt with pick or hoe and then panning it with water. Native mining by the two methods was attested in 17th-, 18th- and 19th-century European records, notably by De Marees, Brun, Mueller, Damon, Bosman, Tylleman, Roemer, and Dupuis. The method used for shaft mining of residual placers in Akyem as described by Roemer was recorded as still in use in Kwahu in 1874 and at Tarkwa in 1877. Major Junner wrote in 1935 that the method employed by Cape Coast women in washing for alluvial gold in the early 19th century, as described by Meredith, was still in use in his day. According to oral traditions the natives also worked gold quartz veins in Wassa and Asante at depths of up to 23 metres in the middle and late 19th century. It is estimated by Garrard that between A.D. 1400 and 1900 the Akan produced a total of about 14 million ounces (400 million gms.) of gold by traditional methods, and that an average of 40 000 miners may have been at work each year when the gold trade was at its height in the 17th century. Of the gold produced, roughly one-third was carried across the Sahara and two-thirds traded to Europeans on the coast.

It was one thing exploiting and possessing gold and quite another utilising it to advantage. It is known, for instance that the Bambuk-Bure gold producers of the West African Sudan were quite happy to exchange their gold for Saharan salt. On the other hand, the great empires of Ghana, Mali, and Songhai used the gold they purchased from the

Bambuk-Bure producers for the accumulation control and disbursement of wealth. This, and the attendant patronage, helped to foster state building. Among the Akan of Ghana gold was a factor in the development of a civilization of well-organized kingdoms, supplied with a currency at home, and all the luxuries gold could buy from abroad. In the past, Ghanaians matched their skill in gold-mining technology with equal expertise in goldsmithery. It is evident from the works of European writers that traditional goldsmithery pre-dated the European advent. For instance, a 15th-century Elmina chief was described as being covered with plates of gold and wearing a gold chain round his neck. John Lok reported that the people of the Gold Coast, 'though they go in a manner all naked yet many of them, especially their women, are, as it were, laden with collars, bracelets, hoops, and chains either of gold, copper, or ivory . . . and girdles of blue stones like beads. Some of their women wear on their bare arms certain fore sleeves made of beaten gold and on their fingers, rings of gold wire' (Blake, J., *Europeans in West Africa*, 2, 1942, p. 343).

Scholars of Ghanaian ethnography distinguish three methods employed by traditional goldsmiths: firstly, beating out gold into thin strips of gold leaf or foil for use in covering carved wooden objects such as stools, umbrellas, royal sandals, crowns, and other regalia; secondly, the practice, especially among the Ga of Accra, of employing cuttlefish bone moulds in the manufacture of gold or silver ornaments by the process of negative casting; and thirdly, the application, especially among the Akan, of the lost-wax or *cire perdue* method in the manufacture of gold crowns, masks, complex ornaments, and sword ornaments.

In Asante, the *adwumfo* or goldsmiths and silversmiths, constituted an ancient class or brotherhood which distinguished itself by the privilege of wearing gold ornaments otherwise regarded as the preserve of Asante royalty and nobility. It is thanks to the *adwumfo* that the goldsmith's art still thrives among the Akan. Ross and Cole's recent publication, *The Arts of Ghana*, provides numerous illustrations of Akan gold objects which are either in private collections or in museums. They are an eloquent testimony to Akan expertise in goldsmithery. They range from gold leaf jewellery to cast necklaces, rings, beads, bracelets and medallions to hollow-cast gold sword ornaments, cast gold maskettes and gold *repoussé* of soul washer's badges.

Technology and art in the medium of wood was a strong point in Ghanaian culture, especially among the Akan, who have been noted down the centuries for their ingenuity in the production of wooden stools, drums, umbrella frames and tops, linguist staffs, architectural wooden panels, frames, posts and lintels. The wooden stool had been adopted as the symbol of political power and the wooden drum as a means of inter-communication, royal ceremony, and musical entertainment, well before Europeans came into Ghana. Wooden stools were described by the earliest Portuguese visitors to Elmina as an important feature of the regalia of the royals and nobility in the 1470s and 1480s. In 1555, Towerson reported a similar trait for the Ahanta chiefs of St. John. A hundred and thirty years later, Barbot described the state drums of the Fante which were decorated with picturesque relief designs. Bosman, who was in Axim at the beginning of the 18th century, said of the Nzema that they made kettle drums by hollowing tree trunks and tying sheepskins at one end, which they beat with sticks or their hands.

When William Bowdich visited Kumasi in 1817, he spoke of the tumultuous welcome that was given him by numerous orchestras and wooden drums and flutes. The fertile mind of the Akan, unable to express itself fully through philosophical and other literary pursuits because of the lack of a fully evolved formal writing, found an outlet of expression in the material media of wood-carving, drum-carving, architecture and similar pursuits. Oral traditions show that although the *asesedwa* or stool-carving tradition was pre-European and Akan in origin, its *floreat* began in the era of Adanse state formation when the Denkyira kings of the 16th century developed the political and cultural ideology connected with the Adanse stool. This culminated in the Asante confederacy institutionalising the stool as the political, social, and spiritual linch-pin of an entire kingdom and, later, empire. Today, Ahwiaa, the centre for stool-making founded near Kumasi by Denkyira immigrants, is still the seat of the Asante stool industry. Rattray's ethnographic study on stools shows that in Asante every stool had a carved symbolic motif which often represented a philosophical proverb of a moralistic, socio-religious or didactic nature. The stool art-motifs like those motifs executed in the media of pottery, architecture, brass 'gold weights', and *Adinkra* textiles constitute no less than communication in the form of a surrogate or proverbial and pictographic script, comparable in essence to the pictographic script of pre-dynastic Egypt and the incipient hieroglyphic of the archaic phase of Pharaonic Egypt. Philosophy and surrogate communication apart, the artistic quality of Akan wood-carving was capable of attaining aesthetically high standards as some ethnographic collections in Ghana's museums and Ghanaian arts centres quite clearly show.

Rattray's monumental study of Akan drum-language is an illustration of how the Akan excelled in arts and crafts during the last three hundred years. Rattray shows how the rich tonal character of the Akan language made it ideal for 'the production of a kind of linguistic music', expressed in the drum language.

In paying tribute to the remarkable development of the Akan drum-language trait, Rattray states in his book *Ashanti* (1923), p. 254

> An untaught African people have grasped and adapted elements in the science of phonetics, in producing a useful means of inter-communication and of practical utility in their daily life; it has helped also . . . to preserve the records and traditions of their past and to foster racial pride in the present and future generations.

Cotton-spinning and cloth-weaving are practised today by specialists in certain communities throughout the country who have acquired their skills from ancestors. Ethnographic surveys have shown that traditional cloth-making is still very popular among the Akan, whose appliqué 'cloth of the great', rich *kente* and stamped *adinkra* textiles are now world-famous. Bonwire near Kumasi is the traditional centre of the lucrative Asante *kente* industry, and at least twelve villages and towns in the neighbourhood of Bonwire cash in on the craft; some combine it with *adinkra*, while others specialise only in *adinkra*-making. In the northwest Brong region around Nsawkaw, Wenchi, Menji, and Debibi, the extant blue-and-white cloth industry has a long history going back to at least the 17th century, when a Dutch map made at Moure in 1629 described the area as noted for its textiles. In northern Ghana and Eweland, local cloth-makers still ply their trade.

The nature and character of traditional architecture in Ghana has been determined largely by environmental resources, the climate, and sometimes by historical factors. In the open savanna lands of the north settlements are of the dispersed large compound or isolated homestead type. Circular buildings are the rule though some rectilinear ones are not unknown. Walls are built of mud or sun-dried brick laid in courses, and roofs either of the conical pitched and thatched type or the flat-earth type built on a framework or grid of timber poles bonded into the earth walls. Among the Dagomba, circular houses with dome-like pitched thatched roofs are common. At Bolgatanga and Zuarungu in the Upper Region of Ghana, both circular and rectilinear shapes, and flat and conical pitched roofs are found side by side in settlements. Elaborate architectural decoration is common among the Talensi, Kassena-Nankani, and Frafra of the Upper Region. In southern Ghana, traditional architecture is of two types. Along the coast, wooden houses with walls of bamboo or woven palm matting and palm thatched roofs are characteristic.

In the forest, however, the tradition has been that of walls of wattle and daub and gable-ended pitched and thatched roofs. Adanse traditional religion has left for Ghana a legacy of indigenous architecture in the form of cult shrines or temples, numbering around thirty, dedicated to traditional gods, like the god Bona Bonsam, of Patakro (Map 3.3). These wattle-and-daub cult houses followed the traditional Asante

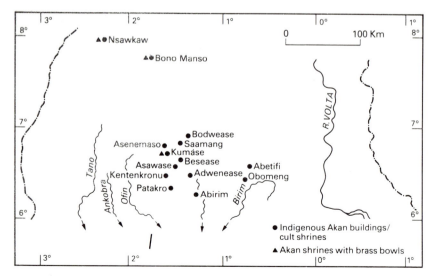

Map 3.3 Akan cult shrines

building style. The plan was cruciform, a combination of a rectangular or square courtyard with separate buildings grouped round it on all four sides, facing the courtyard and linked by short lengths of walls at the corners of the courtyard. Special craftsmen were commissioned to carry out the decoration with timber and moulded mud-plaster. Like all traditional Asante buildings, the cult houses were erected on a raised plinth or base about a metre high. The inner plinth was decorated in red clay with whorls and spirals and the superstructure walls above the plinth were rendered in white clay. Most of the shrines were single storeys but a few had attics. Bowdich's descriptive and pictorial records made during his visit to Kumasi in 1817 indicated that this style of architecture was employed in ordinary domestic architecture and that the Asantehene's palace in Bowdich's day followed this pattern. Thus the cult houses which survive today, but whose antecedents probably hark back to the Osei Tutu period, provide us with but a glimpse of the

Fig. 3.2 19th-century Akan cult shrine at Patakro with symbolic murals illustrating the ram's horn and the sankofa *bird*

splendour of traditional architecture which characterised early 19th-century Asante. Here, priests, moved by traditional drum music, singing and dancing, received and dealt with numerous petitions, including ill health, litigation, female sterility, and witchcraft victimisation. The shrines have very striking mural art depicting symbols like the *sankofa* bird, the crossed crocodiles with a common stomach and the ram's horn (Fig. 3.2).

Recently, the author carried out research at Patakro shrine, probably the oldest of the Adanse cult houses, but housing in any case, the most senior deity of the Asante hierarchy of gods (Fig. 3.3). When the priest of Patakro, Nana Bonsam, was asked about the significance of the ram's horn motif included in the Patakro shrine murals, he replied:

Sir, if you are spiritually strong, so am I, but we can only find out

Fig. 3.3 Patakro cult shrine (Asante) with Akan symbolism. Standing in the middle is Nana Bonsam, current shrine high priest

who is who when our horns confront each other in combat. You shouldn't forget the proverb of the Akan which says that the power of the ram is in his horns, when you break them, then you have him in your power. This is as much as saying that this shrine is a seat of spiritual power and source of succour for the Asante nation.

4   Ghanaian genesis

West Africa is not as fortunate as east and southern Africa in the preservation of remains of early man. Here are none of the limestone caves of South Africa such as the Cave of Hearths and Makapansgat, with spectacular preservation of *Australopithecines* and other early hominids. Here are none of the great Rift valleys with remains of early man and his artifacts and food debris exposed through volcanic and earth movements and through the erosion of fossil lake and river beds which have made East Africa the 'Mecca of African prehistory'. In West Africa, the land has been relatively more stable than in the east. Thus, if the physical remains of early men have not been dissolved in the acidic rocks of West Africa they would probably be buried deep down in the earth.

There is no doubt, however, that man has been living in West Africa for several millennia. The discovery at Yayo (some 200 kilometres southeast of Largeau in Tchad) of the skull and face of a hominid named *Tchadanthropus uxoris* provides some idea of the antiquity of man in this part of Africa. No stone tools were found in association with *Tchadanthropus* but it probably represents *Homo erectus*, well-known from East Africa as the author of the developed Oldowan and the Early Acheulean stone industries. At any rate, both Oldowan and Acheulean types of implement have been found in the same region. Also, the physical remains of *Tchadanthropus* were actually found associated with Middle Pleistocene fauna such as *Loxodonta atlantica augammensis* which may be dated to around one million years. Thereafter, there is a long gap in the fossil record and the next human fossil in the sequence is a Late Stone Age negroid skeleton discovered in a rock-shelter at Iwo Eleru in Ondo State, Nigeria. Iwo Eleru man was found in association with quartz microliths dated by radiocarbon to the 10th millennium B.C. In Ghana, the earliest-known human remains are those of seven Late Stone Age people found in association with quartz microliths, pottery, and seeds of the African lotus plant (*Celtis sp.*) dated by radiocarbon to the middle of the second millennium B.C.

Since human and animal fossils and ancient flora are rare in West Africa, the major 'documents' of the Stone Age prehistorian are stone tools, the chief technological medium employed by man for exploiting the environment and, consequently, the yardstick by which his cultural progress, or the lack of it, can be measured between one million and 2 000 years B.C.

In East Africa, the products of ancient volcanic activity have facilitated the dating of archaeological sites older than 60 000 B.C. by the application of the potassium argon method. Also, relative dates have been obtained by the study of fauna found in association with stone tools. West Africa has produced very few dates for the Early and Middle Stone Age and most of the stone industries on which prehistorians have based their conclusions have been taken not from controlled excavations but from the surface of sites.

One of the notable phenomena of the Stone Age was the remarkable way in which the ocean level fluctuated in response to the freezing or melting of ice sheets and glaciers in the Old world and New world. In general, there was a tendency towards a decrease in ocean level from the Early Stone Age to the end of the Stone Age. Ocean maxima are marked in the archaeological record by a series of raised beaches normally arranged in steps, the oldest being the highest. Some of the beaches contain stone tools. When sea level dropped, rivers flowing into the sea became rejuvenated and began incising their valleys. Prehistoric man also left stone tools in deposits of river terraces. These terraces were previously part of the valley bottom but were left 'high and dry' as a result of renewed incision during a wetter period. In various parts of the world, a study has been made of raised beaches and river terraces and their associated cultural material. In West Africa, there is as yet no agreement on the character and chronology of marine beaches and river terraces. Oliver Davies has advanced a hypothesis of six raised beaches (named beaches I to VI). Beach III is associated with the Acheulean industry, beach V with the Sangoan industry and beach VI with Middle Stone Age industries. A number of geologists have challenged the hypothesis of six beaches but have confirmed the existence of three raised beaches on the Ghanaian coast, the other so-called beaches being attributed to a former shore line which was broken up and tilted differentially. It is quite clear that there have been earth movements and faulting along the Ghana coast. On the basis of field research, Davies has stated that there is enough evidence for the construction of a river terrace sequence for Ghana. In this sequence, the high terrace is associated with pebble tools, the middle terrace with Acheulean, the low terrace with Sangoan, and the inner silt terrace with Middle Stone Age industries. However, this hypothetical sequence has not been subjected to testing in controlled excavations and detailed typological study of industries.

The Early Stone Age

The earliest-known and well-authenticated African stone tool is the Oldowan dated at Koobi Fora in East Africa to about 2.6–2.1 million years. Evidence of the Oldowan or pebble tool industry has been recorded in a number of sites on the margins of the Sahara at In Afalen, Agades, Aoulef, Reggan and the Saoura valley. Oldowan-type tools are said to have been found in the high terrace gravels of the White Volta river at Yapei in northern Ghana and tools said to be of similar type are attributed to sites at Kandinga near the Volta-Oti confluence and in a number of sites in the Birim valley. If these are authentic and can indeed be designated Oldowan, then they represent the handiwork of the earliest Ghanaians. However, a recent re-examination of the Yapei material has cast doubts on it. It would now appear that the stones were so well flaked by the current of the Volta as to deceive the Stone Age expert!

In the African Stone Age sequence the Oldowan is succeeded by the Acheulean industry which is named after St. Acheul in France where it was originally discovered. The hallmark of the Acheulean industry is the handaxe which has been identified at Cape Verde (Senegal), in Guinea-Conakry, at Majabat al Koubra in Mauritania, at Mai-Idon-Toro in gravels of the Forom river and at Nok in tin gravels on the Jos plateau where they have been dated by radiocarbon to 37 000 B.C.. In Ghana, although Acheulean tools have not been obtained from controlled excavations, many handaxes and cleavers probably used for cutting meat have been collected from the surface of sites at Angeta in the Dayi valley, Kwenyakyu in the Ayensu valley, and a number of places in the Volta valley between Akroso and Yeji.

In the provisional river terrace sequence of Ghana, the Acheulean industry is placed within the context of the middle terrace. This is followed by the so-called Sangoan techno-complex which is assigned to the low terrace. The Sangoan is a widespread industry in Ghana. The most diagnostic element in its tool-kit is a heavy pick-like implement thought to have been used for grubbing up edible tubers and roots growing wild and also for wood working. The term 'Sangoan' which has been used in archaeological works of the last three decades to describe this industry is derived from a site at Sango Bay in Uganda which is believed to have produced similar tools. The Sangoan is dated to between 40 000 and 38 000 B.C. at Kalambo Falls on the Tanzanian border. There is lack of agreement among prehistorians working in West Africa as to whether the so-called Sangoan corresponds typologically and chronologically to that of East and Central Africa. Recent excavations at Asokrochona near the port of Tema have revealed a quasi-Sangoan industry of which over five per cent comprised picks, choppers and handaxes (Fig. 4.1(i)) and one grinding stone, while fifty per cent comprised scrapers. Another excavation at Hohoe, a few years ago, revealed an industry in the pick tradition similar in some respects to that of Asokrochona.

The Middle Stone Age

Apparently, following hard on the heels of Ghana's Sangoan, came the Middle Stone Age industry called the Lupemban after a site in Zaire. The Lupemban is generally dated in sub-Saharan Africa to between 27 000 and 12 000 B.C. Its tool-kit includes woodworkers' axes and adzes and bifacial points. A number of parallel-sided, oval-ended handaxes which occurs sporadically in the Lupemban is thought to be a legacy from the preceding Sangoan era (Fig. 4.1(ii)). Some scholars see the Ghana Lupemban, examples of which have been located at Anyirawasi and Achimota, as emerging from a cultural diffusion either from the West African savanna belt or from Central Africa. But its true origin is still obscure.

An interesting industry in Ghana, which is characterised by the tanged point that was hafted and used as a projectile for hunting, has been assigned to the Middle Stone Age although this is not based on excavation and a detailed study of the industry. This industry, called the Aterian, is believed to be derived from the more important north African and Saharan Aterian, a widespread industry of the period 20 000 B.C. to 12 000 B.C. It is named after a Tunisian site, Bir-el-Ater and has produced radiocarbon dates of between 19 350 and 17 500 B.C. at the site of Fachi and Tchad. In Ghana, the principal distribution area of the 'Guinea Aterian' is the confluence area of the Volta and the Oti rivers. A surface collection of 'Guinea Aterian' at Jimam on river Oti has been dated to around 10 450 B.C.

The current trend among West Africanists is to avoid, as far as possible, the indiscriminate use of Stone Age cultural labels borrowed from other parts of Africa. A local term such as 'Asokrochonian' may be preferred to 'Sangoan' for the pick-like industries excavated at Legon Botanical Gardens, Achimota, Hohoe and Asokrochona. Local terms

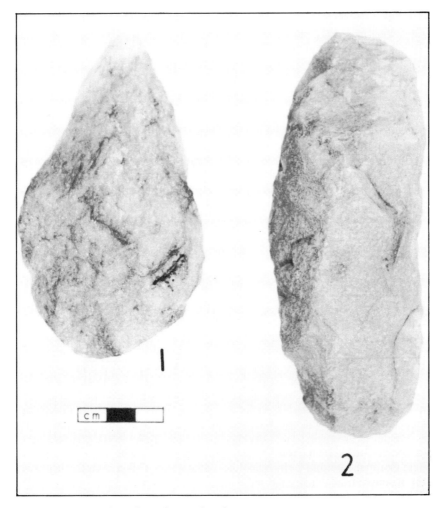

Fig. 4.1   (i) Handaxe from the Asokrochona excavations
(ii) 'Lupemban'-like implement from the Achimota excavations

51

are yet to be devised for the so-called Lupemban and Aterian of Ghana.

In African prehistory, the vast period between the Earlier Stone Age and the Middle Stone Age was marked by important changes in stone technology which affected in no small way the ability of Stone Age Africans to control their environment. The Oldowan and earlier Acheulean men are known to have used the rudimentary technique of direct percussion of a lump of stone by means of a hammerstone. This technique produced a large single core tool. It was previously thought that the flakes which came off this core were at this stage either treated as waste products or else used minimally. However, excavations at Olduvai Gorge in East Africa have revealed that Oldowan and Acheulean flake tools were indeed put to some use. At any rate, the direct percussion technique left deep scars on the core tool which did not make for a good cutting edge. Moreover, the use of the hard hammerstone could only permit partial flaking of the core tool which retained part of the original surface. One of the important landmarks in lithic technological development was the adoption by Acheulean man of the use of a soft hammer of wood or animal bone, or horn for striking flakes. This produced better quality, all-over worked tools called bifaces, and the flakes – hitherto of limited use – now obtained improved cutting edges and so could become an integral part of the tool-kit.

Sometime in the Middle Pleistocene period, the levallois or pre-pared core technique, was invented. This involved careful preparation of the raw materials by taking off flakes round the nuclear core, flaking the top and preparing a platform so as to facilitate the removal of flakes of pre-determined size and shape. The levallois technique thus provided a variety of flake and core tools such as choppers, spheroids, handaxes and scrapers, which were probably the delight of many an Acheulean and Lupemban knapper in Africa and probably in Ghana as well.

The Late Stone Age

At the beginning of the period called the Late Stone Age in African archaeology, the pendulum of lithic technology swung from the produc-tion of core tools, or mixed core and flake tools to specialisation in flake tools. The adoption of a new precision method of flaking called the bipolar punch technique enabled the knapper to use an intermediate wooden, bone or horn punch placed between the hammer and the striking platform of the prepared cylindrical or pyramidal core to produce a variety of long thin blades. These blades could be used as knives without further working, or could be retouched into specialised tool types designed for specific purposes. For instance, a chisel or engraving tool known as a burin could thus be made and be used in its turn in the manufacture of other tools and implements such as needles, harpoons, and spearheads of bone and stone, arrowheads, and projec-tiles. Once the blade technique had been perfected, it was but a short step to the manufacture of diverse microliths by notching the sides of the blades and breaking them.

More is known about the Late Stone Age makers of microlithic implements in West Africa than is known of their predecessors, partly because the Late Stone Age men made use of rock shelters and caves in which stratified deposits are found to be less disturbed than in open sites.

In the early part of this century Late Stone Age sites and other sites which demonstrated the transition into the initial stages of food production and sedentary habitation were studied in the countries of the West African Sudan and Sahel, among them sites such as Blande, Kindia, Kakimbon, Pita, Nhampasere, Petecire, Kourounkorokale, Grotte des Ours and Grotte des Singes. If the impression may have been created by these earlier studies that the Sudan and Sahel were relatively well settled between 10 000 B.C. and the beginning of the Christian era, but that the woodland savanna and the forest had not been successfully penetrated, more recent studies concentrated in the woodland savanna and the forest lands have tended to redress the balance. Among the notable sites of the woodland savanna and the forest whose excavation has thrown new light on the West African Late Stone Age are Mejiro Cave, and the rock shelters of Iwo Eleru, Dutsen Kongba, Ukpa, and Rop, all in Nigeria; Kamabai rock shelter and Yengema Cave in Sierra Leone; Rim open site in Upper Volta; Po river mouth and Kokasu rock shelter in Liberia; Bosumpra Cave and rock shelters of Akyekyemabuo, Tetewabuo, Apreku, and Kintampo, all in Ghana. These excavations have demonstrated that from about 10 000 B.C. onwards, Late Stone Age hunter-gatherers who were fashioning microlithic and flake industries (Fig. 4.2) occupied the savanna and forest and set up intensive food gathering, fishing and hunting economies. From these studies prehistorians now distinguish a 'Late Stone Age' without pottery (B.C. 10 000–3000) and a 'Later Stone Age' (after B.C. 3000), characterised by ground stone axes and pottery. Current research also suggests that the Late and Later Stone Age populations were culturally adapted to their specific ecological zones. For instance, a microlithic population represented at Gao lagoon (about 4000 B.C.–2000 B.C.) in the Accra plains combined hunting with exploitation of shellfish and other fish resources in the local lagoon and riverian environment. In the forest

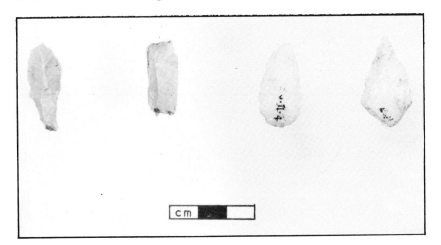

Fig. 4.2 Late Stone Age microliths from Ghana

zone illustrated by sites such as New Todzi and Achimota (Ghana), Yengema (Sierra Leone) and Kakimbon and Blande (Guinea–Conakry), opportunities for hunting were minimal, hence specialisation in the grubbing up of wild tubers and roots using stone picks and hoes. On the other hand, populations of the savanna zone illustrated by the evidence from Iwo Eleru, Rop and Mejiro in Nigeria and Kintampo, Adwuku and Mamprobi in Ghana had a strong microlithic tradition which exploited the animal resources of that ecological zone. There is a school of thought that in the Late and Later Stone Age, the savanna probably extended down to the Kwahu and Kumase regions of Ghana which are now forested. If so, this may well explain the microlithic tradition of Boyase hill area with its unique polished stone arrowheads and those of the Voltaian Scarp of Kwahu, especially that of Bosumpra Cave which has produced rich evidence of quartz microliths, wild *Canarium* fruit and wild oil palm (*Elaeis guineensis*). At any rate, this intensive environmental resource exploitation, coupled with the adoption of the new blade industry and bow and arrow technology as well as the new technology of ground stone axe so conducive to wood-felling in the savanna and forest, and the adoption of the pottery craft so appropriate (normally) for the sedentary way of life – all this prepared the way for the new era of early farming.

5 Pioneers of farming and village life

One of the vital landmarks in the progress of man towards the creation of the ideal society has been the twin development of sedentary habitation and farming. The pages of prehistory as well as the ethnographic record testify to examples of successful nomadic cultivators and sedentary hunter-gatherers in various parts of the world. It is also true that the long prelude of prehistoric nomadic hunter-gathering and its achievements prepared the ground for the emergence of modern man and civilization. Yet of the nomadic hunter-gathering way of life as opposed to the sedentary cultivator's it might be said: 'When I was a child, I spoke as a child, I thought as a child, I behaved as a child, but when I became a man, I put away childish things'.

Human domestication and the domestication of plants and animals were both relatively gradual evolutionary rather than revolutionary developments. Nevertheless, they produced far-reaching results and led not only to the growth of larger populations but also the rise of complex societies and civilizations. The old view of a unilineal development of sedentary habitation and farming in Western Asia and their diffusion to other parts of the world is no longer tenable. Modern scholarship rather supports the view of independent multilineal developments at different times and in different areas of the world. In the case of food production, it supports the view of the domestication of indigenous plants and animals in different areas of the world: southwest Asia holds the credit for the earliest-known domestication-complex of wheat, barley, sheep and goats. On the other hand, the pioneers of New World agriculture domesticated maize and avocados while the Far Eastern nuclear centres domesticated rice, foxtail millet and soya beans and southeast Asia domesticated broad beans and a variety of nuts and vegetables. The new school of thought does not altogether rule out diffusion. On the contrary, there is evidence for regional diffusion of both the central idea of domestication and specific crops and animals. Indeed, the present state of knowledge suggests in some cases inter-continental diffusion, particularly where the continents are close to each other, such as from Asia to Europe or from Asia to Africa.

The origin of food production in the Nile Valley as attested at Fayum, Merimde and El Omari based on domestication of wheat and barley, sheep and goats coupled with sedentary habitation is attributed to a southwest Asiatic source. The idea of cattle domestication in North Africa and the Sahara is similarly attributed to a southwest Asiatic nuclear centre, although it is argued that once the idea was acquired, indigenous wild cattle of the Saharan and Maghrebian regions were domesticated by the locals from the sixth millennium B.C. onwards. In a book entitled *Africa, its peoples and their culture history* (1959), p. 64–65, George Murdock, while willing to accept the view that food production in the Nile Valley of the fifth millennium B.C. had a southwest Asiatic inspiration, nevertheless observed:

> It has hitherto escaped attention that agriculture was independently developed at about the same time by the Negroes of West Africa. This was, moreover, a genuine invention, not a borrowing from another people. Furthermore, the assemblage of cultivated plants ennobled from wild forms of Negro Africa ranks as one of the four major agricultural complexes evolved in the entire course of human history. Interestingly enough, the innovators have belonged to four distinct races. Along with the Caucasoids who developed the southwest Asian complex and the American Indians who elaborated the Middle American complex, we must now align the West African Negroes as one of mankind's leading creative benefactors.

On the basis of modern ethnographic, linguistic, and ethnobotanical evidence, Murdock put forward the hypothesis that food production was evolved independently in the West African Sudan, probably among the nuclear Mande, and that it was based on the domestication of indigenous crops such as fonio (*Digitaria exilis*), bulrush millet (*Pennisetum sp.*), sorghum (*Sorghum vulgare*), cowpea (*Vigna sp.*), African rice (*Oryza glaberrima*), as well as the Guinea yam (*Dioscorea sp.*), which though native to the Guinea coast flourishes in the southern part of the West African Sudan.

Murdock's hypothesis sparked off a great debate among archaeologists and botanists, a debate which is still in progress today. At the time Murdock formulated his hypothesis, radiocarbon dating was still in its infancy and froth flotation analysis for the recovery of ancient plant remains had not been adopted into archaeology. During the next two decades, however, a number of scholars mounted a search for archaeological clues to the origins of farming in Sahelian and Sudanic West Africa, among them Raymond Mauny, Patrick Munson, Andrew Smith, Graham Connah, and more recently, Susan McIntosh. Mauny was the first to study the early farming complexes of Senegal, Mauritania, and Mali and to produce a second millennium B.C. date for cattle domestication in the Tilemsi Valley near Gao in Mali.

Munson's search for the origins of early Sudanic food production led him to Dhar Tichitt, an area in south-central Mauritania whose environment not only provides a nursery for the wild progenitors of indigenous African crops such as fonio, bulrush millet, sorghum and African rice, but also abounds in fossil lake beds that were the favourite haunt of prehistoric people. Moreover, the surface of the site was littered with ruins of ancient village stone houses containing pottery with grain impressions on them. Munson's excavations revealed that hunter-gatherers and fisherfolk of the region, whose culture was characterised by such features as pottery, ground stone axes, sickle blades, and rock art, took to cattle and goat herding sometime in the middle of the second millennium B.C. and initiated domestication of bulrush millet close to the turn of that millennium. This process led to the growth of large villages in the area during succeeding centuries.

Andrew Smith's excavation at Karkarichinkat in the Tilemsi Valley near Gao demonstrated the practice of pastoralism based on cattle and goats almost throughout the second millennium B.C. The simultaneous practice of gathering wild hackberry and other plants as sources of food suggests that if the settlement had continued after the thirteenth century B.C. the events of Tichitt may have been repeated in the Tilemsi Valley with the adoption of plant domestication.

At Daima in Bornu, northern Nigeria, Graham Connah's excavation of a *tell* site produced from the lowest levels evidence of cattle and

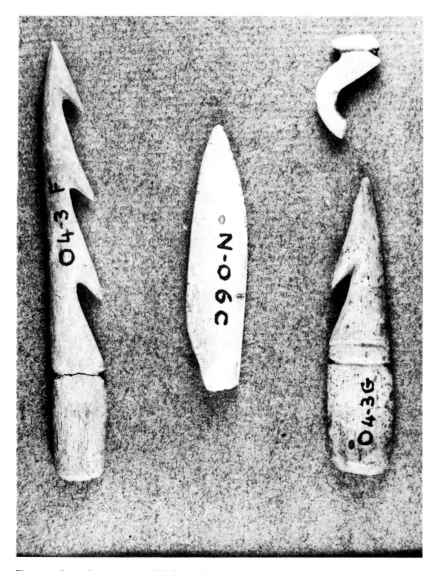

Fig. 5.1 Bone harpoons and fish hook (Ntereso, near Tamale, N. Ghana)

goat domestication dating to the sixth century B.C. Susan McIntosh's research on another *tell* site at Jenne-jenno indicates that cattle domestication was already in progress there in the second century B.C. and that this culminated in the domestication of African rice (*Oryza glaberrima*) in the early part of the first century A.D. and led ultimately to the emergence of an early township at the beginning of the fourth century A.D.

The present state of archaeological knowledge cannot sustain Murdock's hypothesis of an independent development of agriculture by the negroes of Sahelian West Africa as early as the fifth millennium B.C. On the other hand, the evidence is highly indicative that during the wet phase of 6 000 to 3 500 B.C. the highlands of Air, Hoggar, Tibesti, Oweinat, Ennedi, and the regions to the north and east of the Niger constituted a sort of Saharan fertile crescent where mixed negroid and caucasoid Saharan populations initiated the practice of cattle and goat herding. Radiocarbon dating evidence and the zoological evidence of pastoralism from sites such as Uan Muhuggiag, Uan Telecat, Adrar Bous, Sefar, Jabbaren and Arlit bear testimony to this development. Evidence of cereal domestication is also attested at Meniet in the Hoggar during the middle of the fourth millennium B.C. It was probably from this region, then, that the arts of domestication and cultural traits such as pottery, decoration by comb stamping and rocker stamp impression, and typical Saharan equipment such as bilaterally-barbed bone harpoons for fishing and bifacially-flaked serrated stone arrowheads, were diffused southwards into the sahelian and forest regions of West Africa. The available evidence also indicates that once the idea of domestication was known, it was readily applied by the sahelian and forest West African negroes to indigenous crops and animals.

Among the countries bordering the Atlantic coast of West Africa, it is in Ghana that there is available at the moment, satisfactory evidence of early farming. Radiocarbon dates obtained from the sites of Kintampo and Mumute in Brong Ahafo and Ntereso in northern Ghana suggest

Fig. 5.2 Polished stone axes from Boyase hill excavations

that around the early-to-middle part of the second millennium B.C., food production was probably at least partially initiated in Ghana. The evidence takes the form of bones and teeth of cattle at Kintampo and Mumute and bones of dwarf goats or sheep at Kintampo and Ntereso. The identification of the faunal remains from Ntereso and Kintampo as being those of domesticates has been confirmed. Carbonised remains of food plants such as cowpeas (*Vigna unguiculata*), hackberry (*Celtis sp.*) and oil palm (*Elaeis guineensis*) have been found in the rock shelters of Kintampo where they were used as sources of food. Though it is yet to be proved that these were deliberately domesticated, the indications are that these pastoralists were also probably crop farmers. A number of

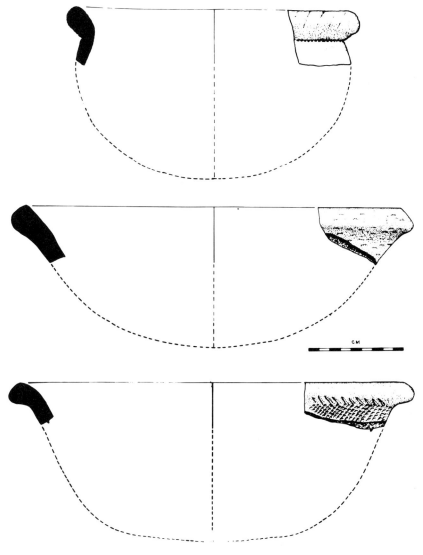

Fig. 5.3 Kintampo culture pottery with comb impressions (Boyase hill)

sites in Ghana have produced evidence of large concentrations of what have been described as stone hoes. These are believed to have been used for grubbing up indigenous white yam and yellow yam (*Dioscorea sp.*) during the later stages of the Stone Age. This practice was intensified and led to domestication between 2 500 and 1 500 B.C. It must be said, however, that inferences drawn from purely technological data are inadequate for proving economic theories related to food production.

The beginning of farming in Ghana did not produce a sudden break with the past. Hunting and fishing continued to play a part in the subsistence economy of the early pastoralists of Ghana. This is demonstrated by the faunal evidence of elephants, hippopotamuses, carnivores, antelopes, duikers and catfish remains found in excavations at Ntereso and Kintampo, the bifacially-flaked stone arrowheads of Ntereso, the polished stone arrowheads of Boyase hill and the bone harpoons and bone fish hooks found at Ntereso (Fig. 5.1).

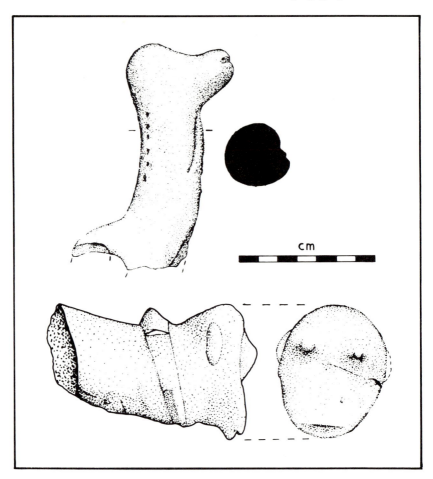

Fig. 5.4 Above: Terracotta figurine (Boyase hill, near Kumasi)
Below: Terracotta figurine (Bonoase, N. W. Brong Ahafo)

As farming is the life-blood of Ghana today and appears to have been so since the second millennium B.C., the material culture of Ghana's pioneer farmers has attracted the attention of prehistorians and cultural historians alike for over a century. In the past, scholars of Ghanaian prehistory used the ground stone axe as the guide-fossil for identifying this culture (Fig. 5.2). This artefact is now known to occur in pre-farming contexts in Ghana, West Africa and several parts of the world and also continued to be in use well into the Iron Age. Today, prehistoric stone axes do not only form part of the ritual equipment of shrines of traditional religion, but are also used by superstitious women who, in search of sexual fertility, put these objects in their bath-water. As early as 1937, Captain R. P. Wild, following the local classification employed by traditionalists for describing ground stone axes, used the name *nyame akuma* as a cultural label for the pioneering farmers' culture and so wrote, for instance, about 'the pottery of the *nyame akuma* people'. However, in line with proper archaeological terminological procedure, the name 'Kintampo culture', which is derived from the type-site, has been assigned to the complex.

The Kintampo culture constitutes a major landmark in Ghanaian archaeology and cultural history. It seems to have pioneered farming, village community life and art, and although the pottery craft is on record as predating farming in Ghana, it is only in the Kintampo culture that potting became a relatively organized industry which may have

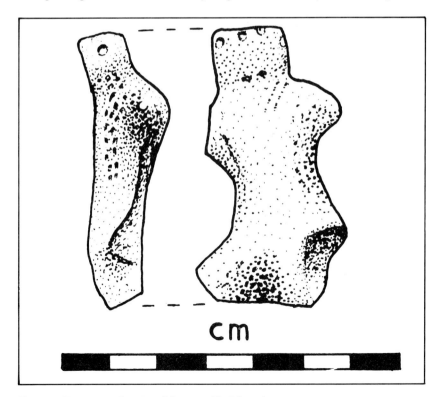

Fig. 5.5 Terracotta figurine (Ntereso, N. Ghana)

been traded to other communities. This may partly account for similarity in the style of Kintampo culture pottery in a number of sites from northern Ghana down to the coast, although there is evidence of some regional differentiation. The pottery forms are simple and comprise wide-mouthed bowls, jars, cooking and waterpots usually ornamented with a comb, either by impression or by a zigzag rockering technique and occasionally by the application of red clay slip and knobs (Fig. 5.3).

These decorative techniques like the rudimentary pottery shapes are paralleled in earlier contexts in the Sahara and the Sahel, a fact which has tempted prehistorians to postulate a northern origin for Ghanaian agriculture and pottery craft. One of the diagnostic features of the Kintampo tradition is the clay or sandstone scored palette (Fig. 2.1) which has been found in nearly every site. Its use is still something of a mystery, though the writer has suggested that it was a potter's tool for shaping and decorating pottery.

Another interesting ceramic feature of the tradition is its art work. Evidence of clay figurines or sculptures which were attached to pots for the purpose of ornamentation has been found in a number of excavated sites. Boyase hill furnished evidence of what appears to be a dog (Fig. 5.4) and a lizard-like creature is depicted on a pot from Ntereso (Fig. 5.5). Specimens of sculptured sheep which have been found at Mumute and Bonoase, like the Boyase hill dog and the representation of a cow's head at Ntereso are of dual evidential value, confirming the development of art as well as animal domestication in Kintampo culture times.

Although some of Ghana's Late Stone Age peoples used caves and rock shelters for temporary habitation, and some may possibly have built huts of grass of which no evidence whatsoever has survived, it is in Kintampo culture contexts that the earliest definite evidence for seden-

Fig. 5.6 Excavating a stone-based rectangular mud hut at Boyase hill

tary habitation and village community life is found. Huts of wood and mud similar to present-day countryside houses of a roughly rectangular shape have been traced in excavations at Mumute and Bonoase, Ntereso, and Boyase hill. The Kintampo culture people of Brong and Asante regions employed stones and laterite blocks for the construction of their hut foundations (Fig. 5.6). Some of their villages, though not large, were quite extensive. Bonoase village may be estimated as about three hundred metres in diameter and Boyase hill as about five hundred metres in diameter. Rock shelters continued to be used as dormitories by Kintampo culture people who occupied areas in the Brong and Kwahu regions of Ghana. Rudimentary village industries other than pottery were not unknown. At Boyase hill, there is evidence of this in terms of stone whose medium was exploited for making hunting equipment such as bifacially-ground stone arrowheads and microliths, wood-working and bush clearing tools such as stone axes, and ornaments such as arm rings and beads. Numerous stone boulders with artificial hollows have been recorded on Kintampo culture sites at Boyase hill, Kintampo, as well as Nsesrekeseeso in Brong Ahafo. During archaeological work at Boyase hill, the area immediately adjacent to a large granite boulder which has several artificial hollows was excavated and produced a number of polished stone arrowheads which have not been found in any other Kintampo culture site (Fig. 5.7). Another trench excavated a few metres away exposed roughouts of stone axes and beads, thus indicating that this was an industrial sector of

Fig. 5.7 Polished stone arrowheads from the Boyase hill excavations

the Boyase hill community. The tool-kit of the Kintampo culture village at Chukoto in northern Ghana shows that they specialised in the making of stone hoes for bush clearance. At Nsesrekeseeso, about 120 grinding

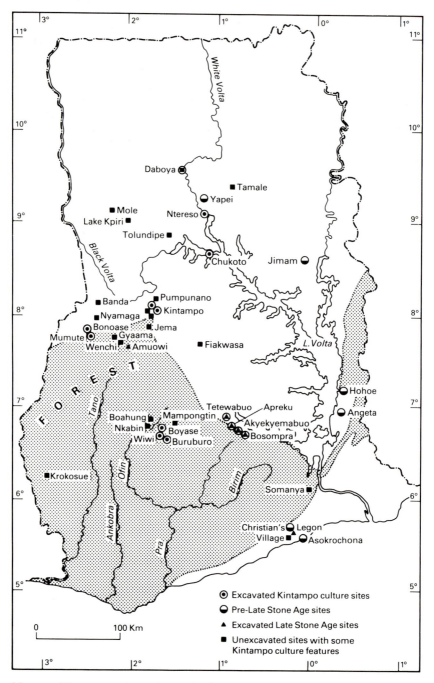

Map 5.1 Kintampo culture sites and other important Stone Age sites

hollows were recorded in a small area inhabited by Kintampo culture people. These hollows probably reflect not only the intensive manufacture of polished stone axes, but also the milling activities associated with intensive food collecting or food production at this time.

Altogether, some sixteen sites belonging to the Kintampo culture have been excavated in Ghana (Map 5.1). Many others are known from surface collections in several parts of the country, including important sites at Wenchi hill and Mole Game Reserve. Sites of the Kintampo culture are found in the forest and in tree savanna and grassland savanna country. There are therefore no real grounds for associating the culture with any peculiar environment conditions. In fact, the bearers of the culture seem to have been very much at home as much with the forest environment of Boyase hill, Wiwi and Buruburo, as with the forest-savanna mosaic of Amuowi, Mumute and Wenchi, and the pure savanna environment of Ntereso and Chukoto.

6   The rise of the metal technology society

Foreign visitors to West Africa from the eighth century A.D. onward reported encountering metal-using societies characterised by complex political, social, and economic systems. In rare cases where some of these societies had copper raw materials or were able to obtain some through imports from overseas, they developed copper or brass technology. Generally speaking, however, iron appears to have provided the chief metallic basis for the technology of these societies. Another metal which featured prominently in some of these societies was gold which became the staple of the trans-Saharan caravan trade and the coastal trade of the early period of European contact.

During the last few decades there has been considerable discussion among prehistorians and historians concerning the *raison d'etre* of these societies, particularly those which showed phenomenal development such as Ghana, Mali, Songhai, Ife, Benin, etc. Some scholars, while recognising the significant role of long-range commerce based on local resources in the development of urbanization and statehood, saw the technological model as the vital clue to solving the riddle of these societies. One such scholar, Basil Davidson wrote in his book, *Old Africa Rediscovered* (1959, p. 83), that 'iron gave a new mastery over soil and forest . . . and an impulse to conquest and centralized government'. Recent research has brought to light evidence of prehistoric copper or brass technology dated to between the eighth and fifth century B.C. in Akjoujt and Lemdena in Mauritania and in sixth century A.D. levels at Jenne, and there are examples of second millennium A.D. copper or brass technology in several parts of West Africa. Yet, the evidence obtained so far indicates that copper/brass was a rarer metal and was employed for the production of special artefacts such as ornaments, ceremonial and ritual vessels and implements whereas iron was the commoner all-purpose metal for making domestic implements as well as agricultural and industrial equipment.

We cannot at present tell how the technique of iron working originated in West Africa, whether it was locally invented or whether it was diffused from the earliest iron technologists of southwest Asia via the Nile Valley or via North Africa and thence into West Africa. The efficacy of iron working depends on the construction of furnaces that can withstand relatively high temperatures. Iron working also involves burning charcoal in the air to liberate carbon monoxide adequate enough for the separation of the iron bloom from the other impurities contained in the iron oxide raw material. Excessive oxidisation resulting from over-enthusiastic fanning from the bellows can make carbon monoxide re-combine with the oxygen to produce carbon dioxide, thus negating the whole process. These pioneers of iron technology were certainly not academic chemists. But these rudimentary basic secrets of iron working were known to them. Scholars who insist on diffusion of iron working from external sources argue that it would have been difficult for the early food-producing people to jump straight from stone technology into the complexities of ferrous technology without prior knowledge or experience of copper technology. Copper occurs only rarely in the natural state in West Africa, for instance at Akjoujt and Takedda. On the other hand, lateritic iron oxides are quite common, hence once the technique had been acquired, iron working was bound to spread rapidly. Fruitless attempts have been made to establish the case for diffusion of the knowledge, either by working out possible routes of diffusion based on evidence of excavated and dated iron, or by the study of old and modern types of iron furnaces and bellows of northern and northeastern Africa in comparison with those of West Africa. Neither has the school of thought for independent invention produced concrete evidence to support its case.

Of greater significance, however, is the hard core of the available archaeological data which shows that traditional iron technology played an important role in the affairs of society. Over half a dozen archaeological sites in West Africa have produced evidence of prehistoric iron extractive industries dating to the millennium between 500 B.C. and A.D. 500, namely, Taruga and Samun Dukiya, Yelwa and Daima in northern Nigeria, Casamance in Senegal, Jenne in Mali, and Hani and Abam (Bono Manso) in Ghana. About two dozen other sites have produced evidence of iron technology belonging to the millennium from A.D. 500 to 1500. These include important sites such as Kouga and Sanga (Tellem) in Mali, Khumbi Salah and Tegdaoust in Mauritania, Begho, Dapaa, Bonoso and New Buipe in Ghana, and Kano, Samaru (Zaria), Ita Yemoo, Benin and Igbo Ukwu in Nigeria. There is an even larger number of iron working sites for the period after A.D. 1500.

There is as yet no agreement as to divisions within the Iron Age chronology. For the sake of convenience the following divisions will be used in the book, namely, Early Iron Age (about 500 B.C. to A.D. 500), Middle Iron Age (about A.D. 500 to 1500), and Later Iron Age (after A.D. 1500). Sites with evidence for the 'early period' in general yield fewer and less sophisticated iron implements. Iron working developed through the 'middle' period and attained its apogee in the early part of the 'later' period after which it declined in the face of competition from imported metal work.

Iron technology in Ghana

In Ghana, archaeological information on the period between the later Kintampo culture and the European advent is sparse and fragmentary. But the available evidence sheds at least a glimmer of light into a period which would otherwise be a totally 'dark age' in the annals of Ghanaian history. The earliest-known evidence for iron working in Ghana comes from an iron-smelting furnace site called Nami at Hani (Begho) in Brong Ahafo. A charcoal sample from the site associated with slag, fragments of tuyeres and furnace structures has been dated by radiocarbon to the second century A.D. Another early radiocarbon date of fourth century A.D. was obtained from the excavation of one of several mounds located at Abam, an iron industrial sector of Bono Manso. The mounds comprise slag, charcoal and other debris resulting from the practice of iron technology. At Bonoso, the nuclear settlement of the Brong of Wenchi, excavations have brought to light an iron-smelting industry dated by radiocarbon to between the eighth and the tenth century A.D. Iron slag was found on the site associated with iron knives and arrowheads and pottery ornamented with comb impressions. The Nami, Abam, and Bonoso early iron working dates, coming as they do from the Brong region which appears on present evidence to have produced a number of other firsts in Ghanaian history, namely, the commencement of farming, urbanization and state formation, show the importance of iron technology in the evolution of society in the Early Iron Age.

One of the important sites in Ghanaian prehistory is at New Buipe in Gonja. The site has produced evidence of iron working in northern Ghana in the eighth century A.D. and thereafter. There are indications from recent research along the Accra plains that iron working may have begun there at an early date. A radiocarbon date of second century A.D. has been obtained at Gao lagoon site east of Accra for what appears to be an iron-using context. Direct confirmation for this is awaited. But there is certain evidence that the proto-urban settlement of little Accra area at University Drama Studio site, which used pottery traded from Cherekecherete and dated to the 14th century A.D., possessed the skills of iron working. From surface reconnaissance and oral traditions, it is known that many other village and town sites in Ghana established iron-extractive industries between A.D. 1000 and 1500. Oral traditions state that before the coming of the Europeans, many Akan farming towns in Adanse built iron furnaces and used local iron called *Atwetweboo* in the smelting of iron. Adanse towns such as Dompooase, Akrofuom, Bodwesanwo and Akrokerri specialised in the making of iron shields and weapons and agricultural implements. Adanse-Edubiase was traditionally the 'Birmingham of old Adanse' and at Adanse Odumase iron ore mines which were worked by traditional methods are still extant. The urban complex of Begho had an extensive iron smelting quarter located near Dapaa. In 1975–76 and again in 1979, Posnansky surveyed and mapped nearly three score slag mounds covering an area of about two hectares. The largest of the mounds are some thirty metres across their long axes and nearly two metres high. Large quantities of slag, tuyeres and furnace wall fragments were found in the excavations undertaken there. Posnansky states: 'The mounds were clearly the result of a very intensive period of iron working and represented a sequence of very many furnaces which had been used and then destroyed with the pieces being thrown on the slag heaps.' (*Sankofa*, Vol. 2, 1976). Radiocarbon dates spanning early to late fifteenth century A.D. were obtained by Posnansky for the Dapaa industry.

In the Akyem Kotoku area, a number of towns, including Abodum, Domiabra, Kokobin, and Manso are known to have striking earthworks characterised by trench systems, banks and deep interior ditches. The earthworks are roughly circular or ovoid and on average are between two and three kilometres in circumference. Settlement mounds within enclosures found in the earthworks are rich in Akan-type pottery associated with polished stone axes, grinding stones, beads, and waste products of iron-smelting. Excavations were conducted on the earthworks at Abodum in 1934 by Junner and more recently at Manso by Kiyaga-Mulindwa who obtained an early 15th-century A.D. date for settlements ascribed to post-earthwork people described by traditions as the Atweafo. It is evident, therefore, that the authors of the earthworks were smelting iron and manufacturing iron implements prior to the European advent. Various hypotheses have been advanced to explain the function of these earthworks. Some have suggested that they were for defence. Others have seen them as labour camps for the exploitation of alluvial gold deposits of the Birim Valley.

Gold industries in Ghana

The exploitation of minerals for long distance trade was certainly one of the vital factors which facilitated urbanization and state formation in the Middle Iron Age in Ghana. Sites of traditional ancient gold mining activities have been located at Jinjini and Chemraso in Dormaa Ahenkro, Nsuhunu, Banda Nkwanta, Senikrom, Awusin and Atuna in Takyiman area, and in a number of Adanse villages and towns such as Kenyasi, Jameskrom, and Jeda. In some of the sites, accessories connected with the gold industry, such as crucibles for melting gold, iron hoes for digging and gold weights have been found together with pottery, clay oil lamps, iron slag, and iron implements. Although most extant ruins of gold mines are likely to be later than A.D. 1600, the foundations of the gold industry were certainly laid much earlier. For instance, the early Portuguese traders encountered or reported on Mande Dyula or Wangara merchants from Mali trading in gold at Elmina. Duarte Pacheco Pereira, writing in the early 16th century, described the gold trade of the Etsi, Abrem, and Akani as being already in existence. Oral traditions of Ayawaso, the site of the 16th–17th century capital of Great Accra, state that the nuclear settlements of the Ga-speaking peoples were mining alluvial gold for export before A.D. 1600 and that it was only later when the Ga found that their Akan neighbours were producing superior gold that they stopped their own production and began to purchase and sell Akan gold. Excavations and radiocarbon dates from Bono Manso indicate that large village or urban sites were in existence in the Brong Ahafo region by the 14th century A.D., precisely the time that oral traditions assign to the beginnings of gold and brass technology, after which this technology is said to have been diffused to the southern Akan states.

Other industries

In spite of the relative importance of iron, copper/brass, and gold in the building of the metal technological society which emerged in Ghana in the first millennium A.D., other industries such as those connected with salt, fish, textile and ivory played a similar role in certain villages and towns. This is to emphasize that not every village or town was engaged in iron working or the gold industry. According to Ga-Dangme traditions, the salt and fish industries were the staple in the economy of the peoples of the Accra plains, from the beginning of the earliest settlements along the coastal lagoons and rivers. From recent excavations at Ladoku, the site of one of the earliest towns of the Dangme, it would appear that a proto-urban settlement with houses built of stone or mud-and-pole flourished on the salt and fish business in the Middle Iron Age and that this settlement was the precursor of a large 16th-century town three kilometres long and two kilometres wide, whose ruins survive till today. There is no direct archaeological evidence for the salt industry at Ladoku but there are numerous *Arca senilis* shells attesting to an important fish industry as early as the 14th century A.D. Whereas Ga metal age society was probably founded as much on gold as on salt and fish industries, Dangme metal age society was probably founded on the maritime and lagoon industries.

The trend of affairs along the Fante coastlands was similar. Local traditions which are confirmed in European written records state that the Etsi people of Abrambo, Eguafo, Fetu, Asebu, Cabesterra and Akoti developed an industry in salt which was traded from the coast through middle Ghana to the middle Niger. In the Brong Ahafo region, an important local textile industry, which traditions date centuries back, flourished in Wenchi and Begho area and its products were sold to the coastal Fante in exchange for salt. This industry as well as an ivory industry – for which there is a modicum of evidence attested in the archaeological record at the Nyarko site of Begho, dated by radiocarbon to the 11th century A.D. – argue proto-urban developments in the Brong region at this time which prepared the way for the major period of urbanization and state formation during the Later Iron Age.

Whatever might be said of the role of various industries in the foundation-laying process of Iron Age Ghana however, there is no doubt that then, as now, the cornerstone of cultural development was farming. In the initial stages of the development of farming, the indigenous white and yellow yams (*Dioscorea sp.*) were probably of major importance alongside the oil palm (*Elaeis guineensis*) and cowpeas (*Vigna unguiculata*). The pre-European cultivation of yams is suggested by occasional descriptions in early European records such as that of Pacheco Pereira, who referred in his records to yam cultivation in the southwest coastlands of Ghana.

A number of the towns and principalities which were founded in the Early and Middle Iron Age have oral traditions which emphasize the role of agriculture in their early development. The Akan, Ga, Dangme, Ewe, and some northern Ghana ethnic groups have extant new yam or millet festivals which oral traditions link with the beginnings of their states. So far, either because of lack of use of sophisticated techniques for retrieving archaeological data or because of the joint conspiracy of tropical climate, soils and soil organisms, ancient flora which should provide direct evidence of agriculture have not been easy to come by. Hence, to infer the practice of agriculture, the archaeologist has had to rely heavily on circumstantial technological evidence in the form of iron hoes and cutlasses, milling stones, and corn cob roulette decoration.

Evidence of the latter has been found in 16th-century contexts at Akroso Beposo and in 14th- to 18th-century contexts at Bono Manso.

In conclusion, it might be said that sometime between the terminal Kintampo culture stage and the early period of Ghanaian state formation, a new society began apparently to take shape. In the present state of knowledge, it will be misleading and, indeed, far-fetched to single out any single cultural trait such as iron technology, gold technology, gold trade, or even the complex of exotic new crops from Asia and the New World as the 'open sesame' to the evolution of the new society. Rather, the novelty of the period is something that embraced all of these and other cultural traits of the period. It is the dual feature of specialisation and exchange of goods. The ideal Kintampo culture family had the potential to be self-sufficient in terms of subsistence economy, technology, crafts, etc. But self-sufficiency became increasingly more difficult to realize in the Iron Age period with its expanding population and its increasing complexity. Already in the Kintampo culture there were signs of some rudimentary specialisation and exchange of goods. The technologist may occasionally have exchanged his polished stone axe, stone hoe, or stone arrowhead for the hunter's meat and the potter may have exchanged some wares for the pastoralist's cattle or goat meat. In the Iron Age, specialisation probably not only became the order of the day, but was systematised and became the *sine qua non* of cultural progress.

The thesis might be advanced, therefore, that it was in the period which some may choose to call 'the dark age of Ghanaian history' that the cultural phenomenon of specialisation was evolved, a vital feature of Ghanaian societies after A.D. 1000.

7 Northern Ghana – from iron technology to Islamic civilization

In many areas of the ancient world, important cultures and civilizations grew up along river valleys and lakes. In West Africa, this is true of the Lake Tchad region, and the basins of the Niger, Senegal, and Gambia. In middle and southern Ghana, the Akan civilization flourished in an area drained by such rivers as the Ofin, Pra, Tano, Afram, Ankobra and Tain. In northern Ghana, the ancestral cultures of the Mamprussi, Dagomba, Gonja, etc., flourished in the basin of the middle Volta. The majority of ancient sites in northern Ghana are located within the valleys of the Black and White Voltas and their tributaries. This is not just because archaeologists have focused their attention more on the Volta valley itself but because these areas, being well-watered, rich in animal life and prolific for farming were the haunt of people in antiquity. Also, the savanna lands of northern Ghana were on the great trade routes leading from Mali and Hausaland into the forest lands where kola, ivory, and gold abounded. The Black and White Volta valleys, and especially their confluence area around Tamale, Damongo, Buipe, Yeji, and Salaga became a cross-road of cultures where influences from Mali and Hausaland flowed into the melting pot of northern Ghana's indigenous cultures.

The Volta confluence area is one of the vital areas in Ghana connected with the beginnings of farming, iron technology, and potting. By the first half of the second millennium B.C. there were established in this area village communities some of which like Ntereso, while maintaining their old subsistence economy of hunting, fishing and food gathering adopted new traits including stock breeding, pottery craft, and stone grinding industries for the production of polished axes, bracelets, and beads. Thanks to the Volta Basin Research Scheme it is now known that by about the middle of the first millennium A.D. there were large Iron Age villages located in the triangular area embraced by the sites of Daboya, Kadelso, and Chuluwasi (Map 7.1). This area clearly had iron industries for which evidence has been found in the form of slag at Owansane river site, while iron implements have been excavated from New Buipe in levels dated to the eighth century A.D. The Daboya-Kadelso-Chuluwasi complex produced red slipped pottery decorated with either comb impression or roulette impression. Painted ceramics, some apparently contemporary with the slipped ceramics, were being produced by communities located within the peninsula region of the Volta confluence. The most characteristic forms of this distinctive monochrome pottery are the *carafe* jar or flask and the carinated bowl. It has been suggested that this may be the handiwork of Guan, Mossi, or Grunsi indigenes.

The rise of towns and kingdoms

The first half of the second millennium A.D. witnessed a phase of expansion in metal technology in subsistence and cash economies and in urbanization and state formation. The story which has been pieced together from archaeological studies undertaken under the Volta Basin Research Scheme (V.B.R.P.) tells of large settlement mounds, the ruins of towns and chiefdoms which emerged during this period. The process of urbanization heralded new pottery traditions and architectural styles and witnessed the introduction of Islamic civilization into the area.

The common occurrence of lateritic iron ore and wood for fuel in the seasonal tropical rainfall lands of northern Ghana was a factor in the rapid growth of iron technology. At least one hundred sites with evidence of iron furnace walls, slag, and tuyeres have been located in

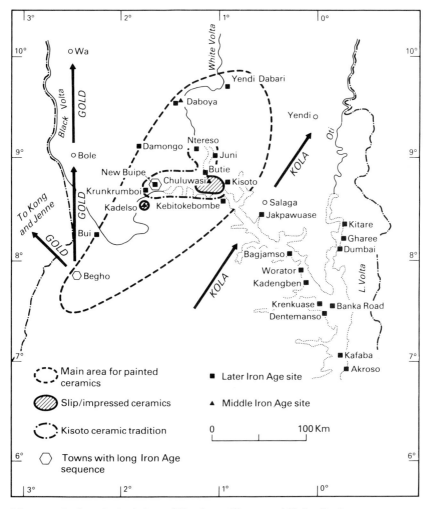

Map 7.1 Archaeological sites of Northern Ghana and Volta Basin

73

archaeological surveys while a number of settlement mounds with similar surface evidence have, on excavation, proved to be the domestic ruins of a versatile iron working populace. Major iron industrial centres which appear to have functioned from around the beginning of the fifteenth century have been recorded in at least nine areas in northern Ghana. In fifteen villages around Wa, there are large heaps of slag and tuyere. Around Salaga, there are at least three villages (the best known being Kakoshie) which have large slag heaps, some measuring over thirty metres across. Five villages around Navrongo (especially Navere and Billaw) have a relatively long tradition as iron working centres. The old townships of Yeji, Bole, Gambaga, Tumu, and Lawra are also marked by many iron slag heaps. Studies conducted since 1900 by geologists, archaeologists and ethnographers have demonstrated that the iron industry was in full operation till the most recent times and indeed is still extant in some places. It would appear that in the crucial period of state formation (A.D. 1300–1800) iron technology was a folk industry *par excellence*, as important for northern Ghana as the gold

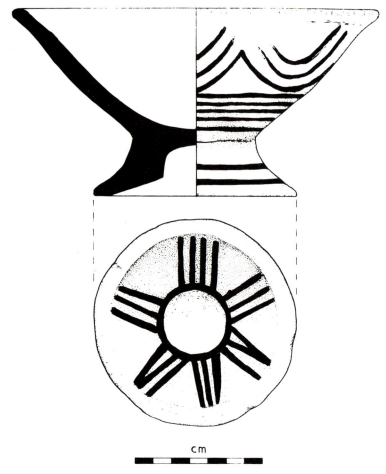

cm

Fig. 7.1 Painted pottery from Ntereso (N. Ghana)

industry was in Akanland in the same period. This increasing tempo of iron technology was an important factor in agricultural production and in population expansion. Southern Gonjaland, in particular, appears to have been so densely cultivated that some areas later became dessicated either through bad cultivation practices or through over-grazing by herd animals and have since been rendered unsuitable for large settlement in modern times.

The role of specialisation in the process of urban development is well illustrated by the historic town of Daboya. Here are many large slag heaps which on pottery evidence seem to be the product of an industry that goes back at least to the 16th century. Here also are large settlement mounds, some ten metres long, full of painted pottery, probably contemporary with the pottery of the slag mounds. It is reasonable to attribute these settlement mounds to the township that grew up as a result of an important alluvial salt industry which is known to have commenced prior to A.D. 1500 and whose products were traded along a north–south trade route that passes through Daboya. Similarly, the old township of Buipe was noted for its pottery, iron, and ivory industries.

The archaeology of the period speaks not only of specialisation in

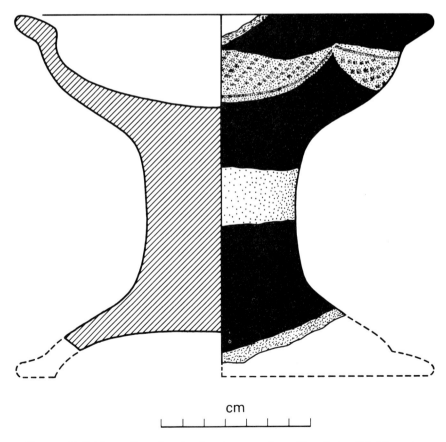

cm

Fig. 7.2 Caliciform slipped and painted pottery from New Buipe (N. Ghana)

different crafts, industries and local economies, but also of stylistic diversification within individual industries. For instance, a striking feature of the villages and towns which emerged during the period was in their pottery. In the 15th century, the Kisoto bowl, a fine grey ware which is named after the type-site, appeared on the market in the peninsula region around the Volta confluence. This ceramic tradition continued in use till the 17th century in settlements at New Buipe, Kisoto and Juni. By 1650, it was a popular 'table ware' in a wide area of settlements. About the same time, northern Ghana's painted ceramic tradition first produced in the Middle Iron Age witnessed further development. A wide variety of monochrome and polychrome slipped wares became ubiquitous in Gonjaland, with their heartland around the Volta confluence (Fig. 7.1). By the 15th century conical and carinated bowls, dishes, jars shaped like pears, jars with handles, and globular kitchen and water pots were common in the settlements. The most

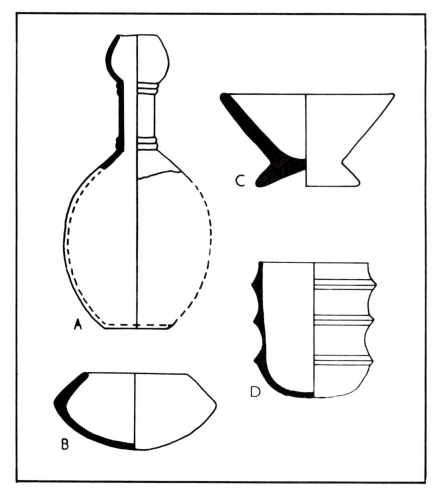

Fig. 7.3 A. Carafe jar; B. carinated jar; C. footed cup; D. trunco-conical jar from New Buipe (N. Ghana)

elegant forms in this tradition are jars with chalice and trunco-conical shapes (Figs. 7.2 and 7.3). Painting as a form of decoration was often executed as an overall coating but sometimes it was executed in linear patterns. In an early variety of this tradition, impressed decoration in zones and incised decoration were executed side by side with design-painting. In a later variety of the 16th to 18th centuries, painting in geometrical patterns and occasionally naturalistic designs was effected on a slip background. It is in its slip and painted pottery tradition that northern Ghana stands out as a cultural area distinct from the regions further south. The southern areas known to have had slip or painted ceramic traditions in antiquity are Begho, Bono Manso and old Wenchi. These southern traditions reflect both acculturation and direct export of these wares from northern Ghana to the northern Akan markets.

As far as can be deduced from the available evidence, the painted pottery and Kisoto ceramic traditions had a local origin. The former goes back to around the 8th century A.D., the latter at least to the 14th century A.D. But in their later manifestations, both wares occur in settlement mounds with a type of architecture that seems foreign to the northern Ghana indigenes. This architectural type has been revealed in 17th-century contexts in excavations at New Buipe, Krunkrunmboi, Kebitoke-bombe, Juni, Jakpasere and Kisoto and has also been identified in surface reconnaissance work at Butie, Kusawgu, Old Kafaba, Larmica and Tuluwe. It appears to have had a flat roof drained by clay pipes, examples of which have been found in excavations. In several cases, it was storied or multi-storied and appears in some cases to have had a tower, hence the name 'Gonja tower-houses'. One of the most spectacular sites with 'tower-houses' is Butie, some of whose fifteen large mounds represent ruined storied buildings with towers.

The wide distribution of the Kisoto and painted ceramics and their association with the flat-roofed tower-houses have aroused debate among archaeologists and historians in recent times. Some have seen their wide distribution as reflecting the expansion of commerce which accompanied industrialization and urbanization during the period. Northern Ghana would appear at first sight to be land-locked and out of touch with the outer world. Yet, evidence of cowry shells found in the settlement mounds suggest that long-range commerce was an important factor in the development of local communities after A.D. 1300. Two types of cowry, *Cypraea moneta* and *Cypraea annulus*, both probably imported from the Indian ocean via North Africa and the western Sudan have been recorded: New Buipe, Krunkrunmboi and Jakpawuase acquired *Cypraea moneta* and probably used it as currency in the period A.D. 1500 to 1700, while Jakpawuase had *Cypraea annulus* after 1650. The Volta Basin Research Project excavation at Bui unearthed the remains of a commercial township located on the south bank of the Black Volta at an important river-crossing on the road linking forest and savanna country. The excavation showed that in the Late Iron Age, materials imported through the European trade, such as European pottery, glass beads, glass vessels, smoking pipes and cowry shells were reaching the northern Ghanaian hinterland.

Some scholars think that the Late Iron Age design-painted wares and the tower-houses may have been introduced from Hausaland and

Bornu through trade and cultural contacts prior to the establishment of the Gonja state. Others have argued that they are direct influences from the middle Niger region, brought by the Ngbanya horsemen and their followers who invaded the area from the middle Niger sometime in the first half or the middle of the 16th century and set up the Gonja political superstructure over the indigenous communities. There is strong pottery evidence which seems to support the middle Niger hypothesis: many large Middle Iron Age settlements and burial mounds at Tegdaoust, Khumbi Salah, Gao, Jenne, Niani, Timbuktu, and the Goundam-Niafounke region have produced carinated bowls, footed cups and *carafe*, *caliciform* and trunco-conical jars ornamented with painted decoration on a slip background (Fig. 7.4). On grounds of ceramic form

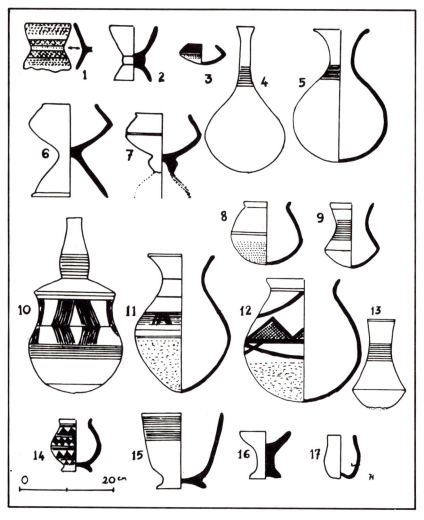

Fig. 7.4 Slipped and polymorphic pottery from Niger bend Iron Age sites (after Raymond Mauny, Tableau Geographique de l'ouest Africain au moyen age, *Ifan, Dakar, 1961)*

and decorative style, their earlier date and their more developed character in the middle Niger area, and the fact that similar pottery influences are evident in the Begho, old Wenchi, and Bono Manso region where the Mande were active, it would appear that the middle Niger played a part in the maturing of a pottery tradition which had begun locally around the Volta confluence.

Gonja traditions recorded in the *Umur Adjadina al Ghunjawiyyin* assert that Wadh Naba, or Nabaga, who founded the Gonja state and became its first king, was originally sent by the chief of Mande Kaba on a punitive expedition against the trading centre of Begho because of a major decline in gold exports to Mali. Naba found Begho already occupied by Mande people so he moved to Yagbum where he set up a military base around A.D. 1554. The Khitab Ghunja (compiled around A.D. 1751) tells us that it was from Yagbum that, aided by the Begho Dyula Faqih, Ismail, Naba launched an army of Ngbanya horsemen against the indigenous people and carried the war of conquest from Buipe area eastward, then northward and westward, reaching the peak of his conquests around A.D. 1600. Naba's successors continued the wars. Indeed, by the middle of the 17th century, Jakpa Lanta (1622–66) was waging wars against Dagomba and as far as the Oti valley. They might have gone further had Gonja not been struck by a civil war followed by an administrative shake-up involving the transfer of the capital in 1709 to Nyanga, the new seat of the Yagbumwura.

Jakpa, known in Kpembe oral traditions as the fifth Gonja king, was as much a nation-builder as a warrior and he actively pursued the task of establishing a political structure for Gonja. In this he was so successful that oral traditions did not cease to applaud his achievements. Indeed, Naba, the original founder of Gonja seemed to pale beside him, and after some time the foundation of the kingdom was attributed to Jakpa. Kpembe oral traditions state that Jakpa's reign is remembered for the palaces of shea butter and honey which he caused to be built at Kpembe, Mangpa, Buipe, and Jakpasere. The ruins at Jakpasere or Jakpawuase near Salaga consisting of a large rectangular complex of buildings (including some storeyed ones) with arched doorways was excavated under the Volta Basin Research Scheme. The large number of iron implements including swords, knives, horses' bits, arrowheads and lanceheads, as well as debris from iron-smelting provide indications of a community heavily involved in iron technology. A comparison of the local smoking pipes of Jakpasere with pipes found in the 17th-century site at Yendi Dabari suggests that the so-called Jakpa shea butter palace at Jakpasere was probably in use in the period A.D. 1622–67. The architecture, which is in Sudanic style, and the design-painted pottery both serve as pointers to the Sudanic belt as the source of ideas of culture and state formation reaching northern Ghana at this time.

There is limited information of the earlier history of the peoples and kingdoms outside Gonja, namely, Dagomba, Mamprussi, Nanumba, Wala, and Gurunsi, among others. According to traditions of the ruling houses of these peoples, they descended from Na Gbewa of Pusiga near Bawku, in the extreme northeast of Ghana. Traditions which are beaten out on Dagomba royal drums state that Na Gbewa was the son of a man called Kpogonumbo who lived and worked in Mali before coming to northern Ghana. Kpogonumbo was in turn the son of Tohajie of Tchad who emigrated into Hausaland before moving to Mali. Gbewa had eight sons. Of these, Sitobo founded Dagomba kingdom, and Yantaure, Mossi and Tohogo founded Mamprussi kingdom. The Mossi state-forming dynasties met older indigenous people north of the Volta confluence – the Fulse, Ninisi, Kipirsi, Kassena, Nanuma, and Konkomba who, lacking centralised political institutions, had evolved looser forms of political organizations, led by shrine priests. In some cases, the immigrants absorbed the indigenes as lower classes of their political systems, but in other cases, they persecuted them thus compelling some of them to emigrate eastward and northward.

The economic mainstay of the Mossi peoples was yam and cereal cultivation and cattle rearing. The 17th century saw the growth of a variety of industries – textile, brass, and leather – and the development of commerce with Mali, Hausaland and Akanland. The resultant prosperity led to the emergence of towns and kingdoms. Traditions state that Soalia founded the Wa dynasty in the first quarter of the 17th century. The old capital of Mamprussi state, Nalerigu, was founded in the 17th century, when a wall was built around the town. The partially extant wall of Nalerigu has been mapped by the Volta Basin Research Project by means of air photographs. Local traditions refer to Na Nyagse as having built a walled town, two kilometres square, at Yendi Dabari, former capital of Dagomba. In 1962, a team of archaeologists led by Shinnie carried out a test excavation at old Yendi Dabari and unearthed the ruins of a large rectangular, and possibly, two-storied building and a walled courtyard. Both structures are in western Sudanic style and quite alien to the present-day architecture of the region. According to traditions narrated by the local Dagomba rulers, the site excavated represents the quarter of Ya Na Zongbila within the 17th-century capital site founded originally by Na Nyagse. Large open enclosures which were brought to light in the excavations as part of the storied-building complex have been interpreted as ruins of strangers' or merchants' warehouses or animal paddocks. Among the discoveries were iron implements and bangles and slipped domestic pottery, comprising fine conical and hemispherical bowls and jars, and large dimpled or footed pots decorated with comb stamping and string roulette impression. On the whole, the pottery evinces a high technological competence. Local smoking pipes found in association with the pottery are in style similar to examples found in 17th- and 18th-century Akan contexts at Begho, Mampongtin, Takyiman and Bono Manso. The Arabic manuscript, *Qissatu Salagha Tarikhu Gonja*, indicates that Yendi Dabari town was in its heyday sometime in the late 17th century and that it prospered from trade linking Akan and Hausaland.

Islam in northern Ghana

One of the outstanding features which distinguishes present-day ethnic groups of northern Ghana from those of the south is their predominantly Islamic culture and religion. Islam began in the 7th century A.D. in southwest Arabia and spread into Egypt and north Africa and through the Berbers of the Sahara into the West African Sahel, Sudan, and forest regions. It was the trans-Saharan caravan trade involving export of West African gold to North Africa, Europe and the Orient and the import of North African goods and Saharan salt which brought Berber and a few Arab Muslims into the West African savanna and forest lands. The kingdoms and empires of Ghana, Mali, Songhai, Kanem, Bornu, and Tchad adopted Islam. Both the middle Niger and the Hausaland–Tchad regions served as Islamic religious and cultural reservoirs from which the more southern states, as it were, drew inspiration.

Between the 15th and 17th centuries, Mande and Soninke Muslim traders migrated from the western Sudan into the Begho area, Gonja, and the Mossi states of northern Ghana, bringing Islam with them. The 18th-century writer of the Arabic manuscript, *Khitab Ghunja*, states that the Gonja royal family was converted to Islam in the late 16th century by two sheikhs from the trading centre of Begho. Abd al Rahman, a Mande scholar resident at Kano, wrote in his *Asl-al-Wanghariyn* in A.D. 1650–51 that Gonja had been settled by Mande peoples. When Islam began spreading in West Africa, the mosque architecture was modelled on that of the West African Sudan, especially the Great Mosque of Jenne built around A.D. 1204, the Jingereber or Great Mosque of

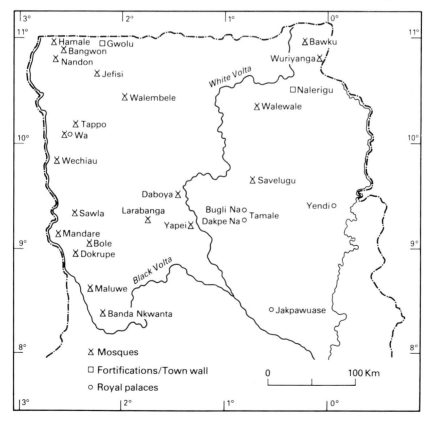

Map 7.2 Monuments of Northern Ghana

Timbuktu built around 1326 by Al Saheli Tuwajjin, and the 15th-century Sankore and Sidi Yahya mosques of Timbuktu.

It has been suggested by some historians that a Muslim group of Mali called the Saghanughu, named after a famous 16th-century Jenne scholar, may have been instrumental in the diffusion of the western Sudanic type of mosque from Jenne to Guinea, Kong, Bondoukou, Bobo Dioulasso, and the Ghanaian towns of Wa, Namasa, and Wenchi. It seems that the Saghanughu found the state of politics following the fall of the Songhai empire not to their liking and so moved into the Upper Niger region. But there they found their pilgrimage route to Mecca blocked by the pagan Bambara. So they contrived to open a new and more southerly route. This passed through a line of towns with Dyula communities – Begho, Wenchi, Kintampo and Salaga – to link up with the Hausaland kola trade route. Everywhere, the Saghanughu are said to have established communities in the Dyula towns, opened schools, built new mosques and revived Islamic culture. Several mosques which date from this period are preserved in northern Ghana as historic monuments (Map 7.2). Larabanga, which is an ancient trading post, has one of the best preserved settlements in Gonja, with two old mosques still extant. One of them, the Friday Mosque, is ascribed by traditions to Ibrahim al-Ansari who was a flag-bearer of the Gonja king, Jakpa (A.D. 1622–66) during his wars against the pagans and was rewarded with the land at Larabanga. A mosque built at Wa in 1801 by Saghanughu from Kong has since been destroyed. Of the mosques built at Menji, Banda Nkwanta, Namasa and Wenchi, only the Banda Nkwanta example still survives and is said by traditional historians to be one of the oldest of the mosques still surviving in Ghana (Figs. 7.5 and 7.6).

Fig. 7.5 The Mosque at Mandare, Northern Ghana

Islam was instrumental in the spread of literacy and Islamic education into Ghana well before Western education began effectively to influence the Ghanaian populace. In obedience to the Prophet Mohammad who commanded his disciples 'to seek knowledge as far as China', Muslim scholars in Ghana began writing histories, biographies and poems after the 16th century with the result that a community of scholars and Koranic schools sprang up around them in towns such as Salaga, Banda, Wa, and Yendi. One of the earliest Ghanaian Muslim works, the *Kitab Ghunja* or History of Gonja, was written in the middle of the 18th century by Al Hajj Muhammad Mustafa of Gonja. First-rate poetry in Arabic was composed in the 19th century by Sheikh Umar Bamba of Banda in praise of the Prophet Mohammad and the earliest successor caliphs. More recently, Al Hajj al-Caghanni of Kete Krachi has written a history of the Salaga war in Arabic and has composed poems denouncing European colonialism and lamenting the decline of religion and morality in Salaga.

The Volta Basin Research Scheme has added to the corpus of knowledge of northern Ghana in the Volta valley around the Kete Krachi region. Excavations at Krenkuase, Ahinkro, Badjamso, and Akroso Beposo have shown that during the period A.D. 1400 to 1800 there was large-scale settlement along the old trade route leading from Kete Krachi to the coastlands. The settlers were iron-using cultivators.

Fig. 7.6 The Mosque at Banda Nkwanta (Brong Ahafo)

Pottery decorated with *pennisetum* (pearl millet) cob was among the cultural material found in the older levels at Akroso Beposo (A.D. 1400–1700). Some settlements engaged in the oyster-shell trade along the Volta and traces of their flourishing business have been found in excavations. The discovery of painted pottery at Akroso Beposo site seems to confirm traditions of Gonja influence and possible Gonja settlement in the River Oti Basin in the 17th and 18th centuries. Local smoking pipes were among the interesting discoveries at Ahinkro (about A.D. 1700), in the upper levels of Akroso Beposo, and Badjamso (dated to around A.D. 1750). It would appear that imported tobacco and pipes probably constituted important items in the trade between the coast and the Oti valley.

However, by far the most outstanding site in this region is Kitare whose earthworks are much more impressive than those of the Abodum and Manso region of Akyem Kotoku in Central Ghana. The earthworks (dated by the radiocarbon method to around the 17th century) comprised three concentric lateritic embankments which enclosed ditches extending over an area of nearly two square kilometres. The site has aroused speculation among archaeologists, especially in regard to its function and date. Several reservoirs for storing water were observed on the site. It has been suggested that the site was probably a trading post which was founded in the late 15th century by traders who carried gold and kola of the forest regions of Ghana to Hausaland and Bouna, and that the earthworks were probably used for accommodating the caravans involved in this long-range trade. It is possible that the rise of Yendi may have led to the eclipse of Kitare.

8 The Akan – 'a golden civilization' in the forest

About half the population of present-day Ghana consists of people of Akan descent. They occupy over half the total area of Ghana. The modern Akan are recognised by a number of distinctive cultural traits: they speak the Akan language which manifests several dialects in Akyem, Akwapem, Asante, Brong, Fante, Kwahu, Sefwi, and Wassa. Every Akan belongs to one of seven matrilineal exogamous clans. The Akan are ruled by kings who are elected on the basis of matrilineal law of succession. The political system features also a queen mother who wields the power of nominating the prospective king for approval by an electoral council of chiefs and elders. The Akan monarchy is a limited one. There is usually an advisory council comprising divisional chiefs who are often also heads of military divisions or *asafo* companies located in quarters or suburbs of towns. Akan societies are noted for their indigenous calendar system which provides guidance for agricultural pursuits, social and political activities. The Akan have a custom of naming Akan citizens from a set list of names according to their week-day of birth.

Akan genesis

In Africa, one of the criteria which have been used in the past for assessing an ancient culture or civilization is the extent to which its origins and influences were attributed by past scholars, rightly or wrongly, to foreign sources. If the achievements of a people were impressive, then they were said to be derived from one of the great centres of world civilization, or were taught, or were strongly influenced, by it. If their achievements were mediocre or unimpressive, then they were regarded as the makings of local autochthones. As greater importance and prestige is attached to the state with exotic origins and cultural influences, traditional court historians quite often distort oral traditional histories to suit their purposes. Thus it is that some works on Akan history assign Egyptian, Western Asiatic, Libyan, Maghrebian, or Mauritanian origins to the ancient Akan. Today, some court historians in towns such as Adanse Akrokerri still trace their ancestry to Egypt or Ethiopia. Great indeed is the temptation to want to isolate certain individual Akan cultural traits and compare them with similar traits in other African or North African or western Asiatic cultural contexts and so postulate major migrations into Akanland. But when the cultural system of the present-day Akan is considered in its totality it becomes quite clear that notwithstanding the introduction of a few influences from external sources, the core of Akan culture is unique to itself. According to Adanse cosmogony, Adanse was the traditional 'garden of Eden' of all the Akan. The name *adanse* means the foundation, or founders of, nuclear settlements. Here, at Adanse, 'the Creator established seven clans at the beginning of time'. In a traditional libation-prayer at Fomena town in Adanse preceding the narration and documentation of Fomena traditions of origin, the local elders and chieftains declared:

> The first of the Akan states is Adanse; Adanse stands at the head of the entire Akan notion.

Other Akan groups also lay claim to autochthonous origin within their own localities, independent of Adanse or elsewhere. The Brong of Hani-Nsawkaw, who are heirs of the commercial metropolis of Begho, state that their ancestors emerged from a sacred hole called *Bonkese*. In a traditional libation-prayer, the Hani chief called on:

> Nana Bonkese and ye Spirits from whom we men originate; all our past heritage has as its head this sacred hole.

The Brong of Wenchi assert that their seven ancestral clans emerged from a hole in the ground at Bonoso near Wenchi after being unearthed by a quadrupedal pig-like animal called *Wankyie*. It was thus at Bonoso that they established their nuclear settlements before moving to their

Fig. 8.1 Adanse Ahinsan chief saying libation-prayers before the narration of Adanse oral traditions

first capital site of Ahwene Koko (old Wenchi). The Brong of Takyiman and Bono Manso have two traditional versions of their origins, one which suggests a northern origin and a second which suggests a local origin from the Amuowi sacred hole. The Takyiman Brong chant at their annual *Apoo* festival:

> We came from Amuowi, ancient Creator;
> Children of Red Mother, Earth,
> We came from Amuowi.

The pottery data from recent archaeological excavations at Amuowi rock-shelter and the application of radiocarbon dating have shown that by the fifth century A.D. peoples in the area of Bono Manso were beginning to establish permanent settlements and to take the first steps which would later on lead to the emergence of the early township of Bono Manso.

According to traditions of the Borbor Fante who inhabit the present-day central coastland of Ghana, their ancestors migrated from Brong Takyiman to Akanmanmu across the Pra and Ofin rivers to the coastlands where they met the Etsi indigenes already established. The horn and drum musical traditions of a number of the twenty-four modern Fante towns as well as Asafo talking drums affirm that:

> Sacred Etsi is from the Creator, Odomankoma; the Borbor Fante met the Etsi already established, and Etsi belongs to antiquity.

Among the Assin of the central region of Ghana, there are oral traditions which attribute the foundation of Akan nuclear settlements at Annow, Bosomadwe, Abakrampa and Abease to the Assin-Etsi. It is apparent that references to Akan ancestral people emerging from holes and caves are but a figurative expression of autochthonous settlement. It would suggest, therefore, that there was a multilineal development of proto-Akan social units in a number of areas such as the northern Brong savanna, the Adanse forestlands, and the Etsi coastlands, and Assin, and that these social groups were probably the descendants of 'neolithic' farmers who spread out to inhabit the forest land between the river Comoe and the river Volta between 500 B.C. and A.D. 1000. The corroborative evidence of archaeology, oral traditions, linguistics and ethnic pattern of this region suggests that it is somewhere in this area that the Akan language and the political and social institutions associated with the Akan must have commenced their evolution and diffused between the Comoe and the Volta. The indications are that the Akan cradle, if there was one, is likely to have straddled the geographical area between Brong, Adanse and Assin, especially since the Brong dialect is known to exhibit some of the most archaic traits of the Akan language.

The environment of Akanland was endowed with rich soils, numerous rivers, large fauna (such as elephants whose ivory made for good commercialisation), iron, the backbone of Akan Iron Age farming, industry, and militarism, and gold, the basis of Akan legendary wealth, power, and artistic technology. Akan culture was erected on the props of agriculture, metallurgy, industry, commerce, traditional religion, and local leadership. But it was, as it is today, first and foremost an agrarian culture. Indeed, some historians of Francophone West Africa have not hesitated to call it such – 'civilisation de l'igname'.

Sometime between 2000 B.C. and 1000 B.C. farming began in areas which are today inhabited by Akan-speakers. Ruins of stone-using village communities which probably kept livestock and perhaps also cultivated crops are known in Brong Ahafo and Asante regions. Oral traditions narrated by modern Akan living in these areas say their ancestors used ground stone axes and hoes (the hallmark of the early farming sites) which they call *Nyame akuma* (God's axe) for digging and woodworking (Fig. 5.2). These areas of Akanland in Brong and Asante where there is evidence of stone-using farming communities have also produced archaeological and oral historical evidence of the pioneering of Akan town life and state formation. Akan oral traditions are explicit that the development of farming was accompanied at an early date by the institution of an indigenous calendar (*Akanfoo asranaa ne nna bone*), in which every day of the year was named and listed and was used as a guide for the agricultural cycle of ground preparation, sowing, and harvesting and also for observing local traditional festivals and other social customs. The development of the Akan child-naming system referred to above was based on this calendar which is now published and used alongside the conventional western calendar. The Akan calendar, which is based on observation of the constellations, provides evidence of the local initiation of 'science' in prehistoric times though serious cognizance has not been taken of it because it was not generally executed in conventional writing. It is interesting, however, that when Pieter de Marees visited the Elmina area in 1601, he recorded parts of the traditional Fante calendar which was then in use.

Contemporary experience shows that society cannot successfully develop from the family level through the tribe to the city-state, then to the nation-state or to the level of empire without undergoing techno-logical changes which bring about increased production in agriculture and industry. Axes and hoes with stone heads and wooden handles were adequate tools for tree-felling and cultivation for a few score people in the second and first millennium B.C. forestlands of Ghana. It was quite another matter where large populations were concerned. For them, agricultural production had to undergo major changes which could come not only from improvement in farming techniques and introduc-tion of new crops and livestock but also, and probably initially, from major changes in technology. As already shown in Chapter 6, iron working was known in the Brong region in the first half of the first millennium A.D. During the Middle and Later Iron Age, it became increasingly widespread in Akanland. Bono Manso capital site, for instance, had an industrial quarter which supplied iron for agricultural, industrial and military needs. Excavation of house mounds belonging to different phases of the town from A.D. 1250 to 1750 brought to light a variety of iron goods – spoons, knives, bracelets, needles, and arrow-heads. When Ahwene Koko, capital site of old Wenchi, was dug up recently by an archaeologist, iron slag and iron implements were among the discoveries dated by radiocarbon to the 16th century. A decade of intensive archaeological research at Begho has shown that between A.D. 1400 and 1750 the town was turning out large quantities of iron work. Over two thousand implements have been found in excavated settlement mounds, a large number of smelting furnaces have been located at Dapaa, a suburb of Begho, and an ironsmithing shop has been excavated at the Dwinfuo quarter of Begho. Evidence of iron technology has been found in ruins of Akan communities at Beifikrom, the earthwork complex of Akyem, the 16th-century Asebu town site and at Cape Coast. In general, the period of greatest development of iron technology A.D. 1300–1700 was also the period of major urban and state development among the Akan.

The golden civilization

Industry and commerce constituted twin factors of importance in early Akan development. In particular, the gold industry featured prominently in Akan economy from the 14th century.

Oral traditions of some of the Akan attest to the vigorous development of the gold industry in the Middle and Late Iron Age. Edina (Elmina) traditions state that the original founder of the state, Kwaa Amankwaa of Eguafo, chose the site at Edina because he found alluvial gold on the banks of the local river and so named the river 'Menya' (later corrupted to 'Benya'), meaning, 'I have found a treasure'. Court historians of Akatakyi (Kommenda) and Abrem state that their lands were a rich source of gold which was exploited in the early European period in Fanteland. According to traditions of the Wenchi area, gold was panned in or near rivers and streams, among others, the Tain, Bisi, Atom, Adaagye, and Botim. The gold was dug up by the men and the women washed it. Goldsmiths then melted down the gold for the manufacture of gold and jewellery. Similar traditions have been documented for Adanse and Bono Manso.

The records of several European writers give support to the traditional histories. A Venetian map of about 1489 described Ahanta state as 'extending for seven or eight leagues, containing a gold mine yielding 20,000 doublons or more; the gold is taken to be bartered at St. Jorge de Mina Castle' (G. Kimble [ed.], *Esmeraldo de situ orbis*, London, 1937, p. 118).

Antonio Proes who was governor of Elmina, in a letter of 19 August 1513, addressed to the king of Portugal, complained bitterly of 'gold being drained away from the coast through this Mandingua leak which was never so gaping as at present' (Teixeira da Moto, *Manding Conference Papers*, 1972, p. 118). Duarte Pacheco Pereira, governor of Elmina castle from 1513 to 1522, wrote in the *Esmeraldo de situ orbis* that negro merchants who brought good quality gold to Elmina castle from distant lands included the Bermus (Abrem), Atis (Etsis), Hacanys (Akanni), Boreoes (Abura), and Mandinguas (Mande). Pieter de Marees described gold mining and smithing industries in the Elmina area in 1601. A map which was drawn by an anonymous Dutch cartographer at Moure on Christmas day, 1629, provides some idea of the distribution of gold mining and gold trading centres in Akanland at the time (see Map 8.1).

Map of the regions of the G.C. in Guinea as we have enquired on various places on these coasts from the most experienced Blacks and so far as our nation visits here (this region) ordinarily and have ourselves also experienced (found).

This for the first time so gathered brought together in the interest of those who take speculation in her, till by somebody else a better one will be made.

Done this 25th December 1629 in Guinea at Moure

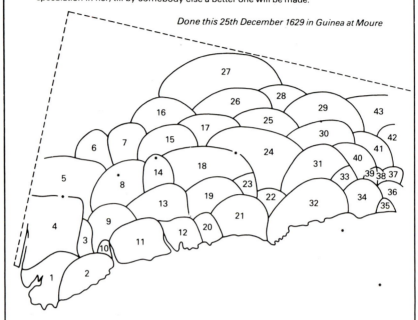

1 Cabo de Tres Puntas
2 Anta (Coast:W-E:hamlet, fishing village, Beturij, Papompando, Aioba, Tacorarij or Anta, Maquesanquie? Saconde, Boarij, cama.)
3 Mampa, rich in gold
4 Igwijra, Rich in gold
5 Great Inkassa
6 Incassa Igwijra
7 Wanquie have gold, and they are merchants
8 Wassa, very rich in gold
9 Adom, merchants
10 Sabeu
11 Commendo or Guoffo. (Coast,W-E: Cocoberij, Aborbij, good fishing-village, Aytaque or Little Commendo, Ampea, salt-village, saltvillage Mijna).
12 Futu (Coast W-E: hamlet, saltvillage, Cabocors).
13 Abramboe
14 Kuiforo
15 Bonnoe. Simple people. No forest.
16 Nil
17 Inta

18 Acanij. Here live the most principal merchants who trade gold with us.
19 Atij
20 Saboe. (Coast, W-E: salt-village, Moure, salt-villages)
21 Fantijnn. Coast, W-E: Iron bush, Don Pedro's village, saltvillage, Anamabo, Planters' village. (Potters' cachalot?) saltvillage, Cormantijn, Mijna-fishers, Rio Amijsa, saltvillages, Mijna fishers, Rio Indaco, saltvillage, saltvillages.
22 Sonquaij
23 Aqua
24 Akan or Great Akanij. Very delicate people, and rich in slaves
25 Akan
26 Nil
27 Insoco. There is no gold, nor trade from there, but they have very fine goods. Clothes woven like carpets which are worn (?) amongst the Acanists. Have also horses. Live in fortifications, but don't have firearms.

28 Nil
29 Tafoe. Rich in gold
30 Quahoe, rascal-people
31 Aquemboe. Thievish people.
32 Agwano or the country of Janconcomo very prone to war (Coast W-E: savage corner, (rough cape), Mijna fishers, Polderbay, Devil's Mountain, New Bijamba, Old Bijamba, Barcu, Jaco, Cox broot, Little Barcu
33 A,B,C, the market of Acara
34 Great Acara. (Coast W-E: Socho, Momboribij, Acara, Orsou).
35 Labade
36 Ningo
37 Latabij
38 Equea
39 Boenoe
40 Aboera, has gold.
41 Kammana
42 Arcarady - much gold
43 Quahoe. Rich in gold

Map of the Gold Coast translated from the Dutch

Map 8.1 *The Gold Coast in the 17th and 18th centuries*

The map indicates the main gold areas as follows:

Aboera – has gold.
Akanij – here be the most principal merchant who trade with us.
Arcarady (Akyem) – much gold.
Quahoe (Kwahu) – rich in gold.
Tafo – rich in gold.
Wassa – very rich in gold.
Wanquie (Wenchi) – have gold and they are merchants.

In 1668, Olfert Dapper described the gold industries of Akyem, Akanni, Axim, and Kwahu whose products were traded down to the coast. W. J. Mueller noted in 1673 that the pre-Asante principalities of Tafo and Kase in Adanse had deep gold mines which were prolific. In 1760, F. L. Roemer provided a vivid description of the processes of Akyem gold mining technology. He noted that gold was extracted from pits dug in the ground in a slanting manner. The pits looked like a staircase with each step measuring about a metre high. On each step stood a man who passed up trays full of soil and passed down the empty ones, while workers at the bottom of the pit picked the ore loose and filled the trays. The depth of the pits varied between 4 metres and 10 metres but occasionally a pit was found that exceeded 50 metres. The simple implements which were employed in the industry were described by

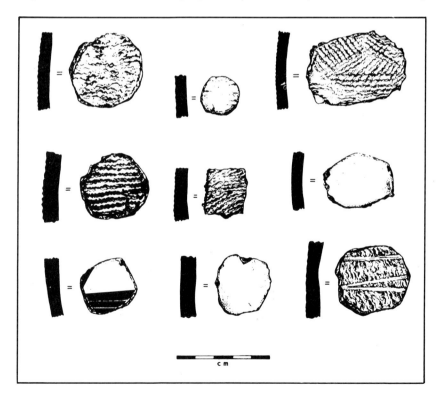

Fig. 8.2 Pottery discs from excavations at Begho (N.W. Brong Ahafo) probably used as gold weights

19th-century Basel missionaries as including a long-bladed spud for digging, a wooden bucket for baling out water or for hoisting up the earth containing gold, and a bowl for washing the gold.

During the last few decades, many old gold mining sites worked by traditional methods have been discovered and studied by geologists, archaeologists, and historians alike in Brong, Adanse, and Fanteland. In his monograph series on Fante oral traditions, the historian John Fynn refers to numerous old gold pits of Abrem which were worked in antiquity and for which evidence is extant today. In some of the sites in Adanse and Brong Ahafo, traditional equipment for the industry have been found together with pottery, iron implements and slag. At Begho and Bono Manso, evidence has been found of well-shaped rectangular or circular pottery discs or stones (Fig. 8.2) which have been systematically weighed by a metrologist, Timothy Garrard, and found generally to correspond to the Western Sudanic Islamic weight sytem believed to have been adopted by the Akan for weighing gold. Gold ornaments – rare archaeological discoveries in Ghana – have been retrieved from sites such as Dawu in Akwapem, Efutu in Fanteland, and Twifo Hemang in Assin. They show that the early Akan were not satisfied with merely exporting the raw gold but that they set up small-scale manufacturing industries based on gold. These were the forbears of the highly centralized industries which operated under the patronage of the Asante kings of the 18th and 19th centuries. It is not without justification therefore, that francophone West African historians thus impressed have described Akan as 'civilisation de l'or' – the golden civilization.

Apart from gold, other specialist industries grew up in Akanland whose products facilitated both short and long range commerce and provided the stimulus for urban and state development. Oral traditions of Kommenda and Elmina speak of locals manufacturing salt by boiling salt water from the coastal streams which enter the Atlantic ocean. The salt was exported together with roasted fish by *batafo* (merchants) in *apakan* (wooden trays) to other Fante states and as far as Adanse, Wassa and Brong Ahafo. The Dutch map of Moure (1629) draws attention to the salt and fishing business among the Fante coastal states of Asebu, Cormantin, Efutu, Elmina, Eguafo and Kommenda. In the Brong region, oral traditions indicate that local industrial specialization expressed itself in the development of textiles, ivory and copper or brass crafts, especially in the Hani-Nsawkaw, Bono Manso–Takyiman and Wenchi areas. While Olfert Dapper noted the popularity of 17th-century Wenchi textiles, the Dutch author of the 1629 map stated that the Nsawkaw (Begho) area was famous for its 'very fine goods – clothes woven like carpets which are worn'. This is strongly supported by local traditions which state that '*yede Beo ntoma twa mpoa*', meaning the wealthy used their rich Begho cloths in casting insinuations on the less affluent. Excavations have brought to light numerous spindle whorls and dye holes attesting to local cloth manufacture at Begho and Bono Manso between the 14th and the 18th centuries and at Wenchi in the 16th and 17th centuries. Ivory industries appear to have commenced in the Begho area from the beginning of the second millennium A.D. reaching their *floruit* around the 15th and 16th centuries when ornate court ivory trumpets were carved. Archaeological contexts at Bono

Manso dated to between the 15th and 17th centuries prove the existence there of ivory ornamental industries. The archaeology of the Brong area seems to lend support to oral traditions which state that the Brong were experts in brass casting in pre-Asante times and that Asante acquired its brass casting skills from Brong Ahafo.

Sites in all three areas – Begho, Bono Manso and Wenchi – have yielded locally-made brass or copper bracelets, knives, spoons, and needles. The author's excavation at the *Dwinfuo* or artisans' quarter at Begho revealed a copper or brass foundry containing large fragments of broken hearths or furnaces, at least 500 clay crucibles used in the melting of copper, numerous sherds of industrial pottery, as well as actual manufactured brass goods (Fig. 1.6). However, the results of Thurstan Shaw's excavation at Dawu clearly demonstrate that the early

Fig. 8.3 16/17th century jug from the Rhine, W. Germany, excavated from Akan grave at Bokuruwa (Kwahu), in the Institute of African Studies Museum, Legon

development of specialist industries in textiles, ivory and brass was not confined to the northern Akan but that the southern Akan of Akwapem also developed similar industries. The large midden at Dawu dated to *c.* A.D. 1550–1700 threw up ivory combs and bracelets carved with delicate finesse in diverse motifs, spindle whorls used in spinning cotton, moulds and crucibles used in *cire perdue* casting of copper vessels and jewellery and brass objects.

The Akan organized long range trade with the middle Niger regions along the northwest trade route leading to Jenne, with Hausaland along the northeast trade route, and with the European nations along the coast. Akan commerce was organized by local merchants referred to as *batafo* both in oral traditions and in European written records such as Pieter de Marees's work of 1601. Akan items of trade included gold, ivory, kola and slaves which were exchanged for imported textiles, metal ware and metal bars, foreign pottery, ornaments, guns, cowry shells, smoking pipes, tobacco and drinks. This led to the introduction of external ideas and materials into Akanland – crops and animals from the New World and Asia, new religions, new technological, cultural and artistic traits. Evidence of European-imported objects such as pottery, smoking pipes, glass beads, and cowry shells has been found in excavations in several sites known from European records and oral traditions to have been occupied by the ancient Akan – Asebu, Efutu, Elmina, Kommenda and many sites adjacent to European forts and castles in Fanteland, at Abotakyi and Dawu in Akwapem, at Mampongtin and Ahinsan in Asante; Bono Manso, Takyiman, Tanoboasi, Ahwene Koko, and Begho in Brong Ahafo (Figs. 8.3 and 8.4). At Begho,

Fig. 8.4 Imported piece of brass bowl from 17th-century settlement of Ahwene Koko, Wenchi (Brong Ahafo), Institute of African Studies Museum, Legon

archaeologists found an intriguing specimen of a 17th-century Chinese piece of porcelain (Fig. 8.5). At Nsawkaw, there are cult shrines in which brass bowls with Arabic inscriptions on them are used as receptacles for the deities. Three such bowls studied by the arabist, John Hunwick, bear Arabic *kufic* or *naskh* inscriptions in the style of Mameluke Egypt of the 14th and 15th centuries. It would appear that these vessels were traded south from North Africa through the West African Sudan.

There are few remains of old towns, town life and states in the forest and woodland inhabited by the Akan. Thus little headway can be made by the sole use of archaeology in reconstruction of past developments in state building without recourse to correlational evidence of written evidence, oral traditions and ethnography.

It used to be said by historians of the 1950s and 60s that the advent of Islamic and European civilization was instrumental in the development of towns and states in West Africa and that urbanization was unknown in pre-Islamic times. The findings of the most recent research in the Sudan as well as the forest is contrary to this view. It is now known that by the third century A.D. a walled town which extended half a

Fig. 8.5 17th-century Chinese porcelain from excavations at Begho (Brong Ahafo)

kilometre across had developed at old Jenne, probably out of local trade and agricultural wealth. It is also known that during the second quarter of the second millennium A.D. and prior to the European advent, towns had begun to emerge in the area of Bono Manso and Begho and in Dangme country of the Accra plains in response to local developmental factors.

The period A.D. 1000 to 1400 seems to have witnessed the emergence of the earliest towns and principalities with centralized political authority and social institutions in the Akan areas of Asebu, Ahanta, Fetu, Elmina, Abrem, Kommenda, Adanse, Twifo, Bono Manso, and Begho. The hinterland kingdom of Acames (Acanni) already existed by the 15th century and a Portuguese governor of Sao Jorge at Elmina on his appointment established diplomatic relations with Acames and sent gifts to its king. Typical Akan regalia associated with statehood such as the wooden stool, drums, ivory trumpets and military array were on display when Diego d'Azambuja, the Portuguese captain who built Elmina castle, met King Caramansa of Edina and his court elders in 1482. One of the fruits of recent intensive studies into Fante oral traditions is a king-list of the Edina dynasty founded by Kwaa Amankwaa. The list contains the names of thirty-one monarchs or regents who have occupied the Edina throne to the present-day, five of whom, Kwaa Amankwaa, Kwesi Djan Ansah, Ampon Kumah, Ebo I and Kobina Amankwaa preceded Kwamina Ansah who was the reigning monarch at the time Elmina castle was built. It is evident, therefore, that the Edina monarchy and the polity associated with the stool were first established prior to the European advent.

Recent archaeological investigations have shown that in the Bono Manso and Begho areas, there are numerous settlement mounds which vary in size according to their function and position in the chronological sequence and so provide some idea of urban development. At Bono Manso, two main periods of town development have been distinguished. The first period, spanning the 13th and the 15th century, is marked by relatively smaller scattered mounds containing less evolved pottery. The main period, spanning the 15th and the late 17th century, is represented at some eleven sites altogether and is marked by larger and more comprehensively distributed mounds containing diversified pottery styles, European imports and local smoking pipes. At its peak in the 17th century, the capital site extended over an area of two kilometres square and its population was probably around 5 000. It was the seat of the Bono king and also the chief commercial and industrial centre. It had seven satellite villages superintended by sub-chiefs who were also provincial rulers over tributary principalities such as Amoman, Asekye, Dewoman, Nyafoman, and Takyiman. There were also a number of trading centres at Kramokrom (Muslim town), Forikrom, Ameyaw-krom, and Sempoakrom (Map 8.2).

Oral traditions of Hani and Nsawkaw locate the nuclear settlement of Begho at Nsesrekeseeso first established by chief Kutu and queen mother, Bene. The traditions state that he was assisted in his government by officials who had stools of office. Begho's subsistence economy combined cereal and root crop cultivation (namely, millet, rice and yam) with cattle rearing. This was to be expected in an environment which was transitional between the forest and the savanna. Alluvial gold was obtained from the river Koosono and was exported. The beginnings of Begho township may be associated archaeologically with an 11th-century settlement whose foundation is attributed by local traditions to a legendary founder called Efua Nyarko. The Nyarko site has large concentrations of pottery with diverse styles extending over half a mile square. The town grew up during the next five centuries, attaining its apogee sometime in the 17th century when it covered an area of eight kilometres by five kilometres and had a population which has been estimated by Merrick Posnansky – on the basis of the distribution of ruins of houses and the density of their archaeological contents – at around 7 000. The town had a number of suburbs or quarters named by local traditions and these were involved in specialist activities (Map 8.3). The Brong quarter was the seat of the Akan chief and the nerve centre of the town. The *Kramo* or Muslim quarter almost certainly had a

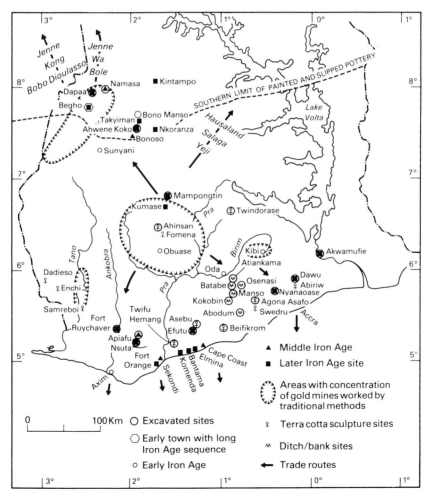

Map 8.2 Archaeological sites of Akanland

central mosque built of mud which may have disappeared without a trace in the archaeological record. The *Dwinfuo* or artisans' quarter was the focus of a complex of copper and ironsmithing industries. There was a *Dwabirim* or central market as well as an iron-smelting centre.

The archaeological evidence argues vigorous industries – cloth making, ivory carving, potting, brass working, and iron working. Some of the products, especially cloths and pottery were traded in various directions. Late Iron Age pottery manufactured at Begho has been excavated in contemporary settlements at Bono Manso and old Wenchi, while pottery from Bono Manso has been found in the settlements at Begho. Begho's export of gold and kola to the middle Niger region through the agency of Mande merchants who dwelt in the town's *kramo* quarter was probably reciprocated with the importation of North Afri-

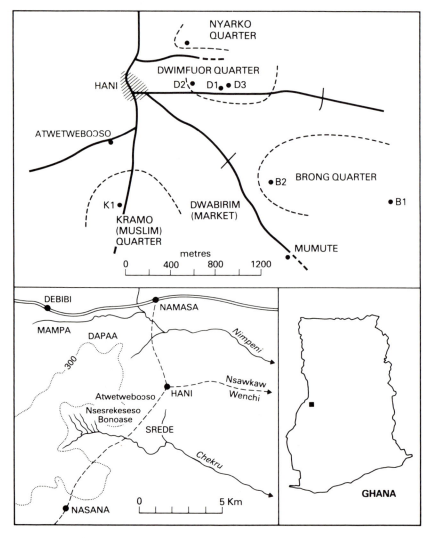

Map 8.3 Archaeological sites of Begho

Fig. 8.6 Bronze jug of 14th-century English King Richard II, from Kumasi (Asante)

can brassware, oriental porcelain and horses. Begho oral traditions indicate that Kutu and his successors thought it prestigious to ride on horses. Some substantiation for the traditions was found in the discovery of horse bones during excavations in the Brong quarter of Begho. Southern Akan groups came to Begho with European goods, salt, fish, gold and kola and this probably accounts for the presence at Begho of European pottery, Dutch and Venetian glass beads and cowry shells. Nearly one thousand smoking pipes have also been excavated from the Begho mounds. This may suggest that unless local smoking weeds were in use, tobacco was probably one of the major imports which entered Begho from the Atlantic coast as Muslims from the middle Niger were most unlikely to have engaged in the tobacco trade.

In most parts of Akanland, the period A.D. 1500 to 1800 was the high-water mark of urbanisation and state formation. The 1629 Dutch map of Moure refers to some 29 states including Akan states such as Akwamu, Akyem, Agona, Asebu, Ahanta, Bono, Gyaman, Kommenda, Kwahu, Nsawkaw, Wassa and Wenchi. There were doubtless many more which were left unrecorded by Europeans at the time. Towerson wrote in 1556 – though not without some exaggeration – that the walled town of Fetu was 'by the estimation of our men as big in circuit as London' (Blake, 1942, p. 406). Excavations at Asebu have revealed that commerce was an important factor in the expansion and prosperity of the kingdom. Evidence from Bokuruwa in Kwahu, Dawu, and Abotakyi in Akwapem, and Nyanaoase in Akwamu proves beyond all doubt that trade after 1500 did stimulate state formation in Akanland. From archaeological sites in these areas and sites such as Mampongtin in Asante and Ahwene Koko and Tanoboase in Brong European imported goods have been found.

Arts and crafts of the Akan

In the past, historians have relied on written records which tended to concentrate on politics and economics to the exclusion of social, artistic and ideological matters. Recent comparative archaeological and ethnographic research has shed new light on the immediate past of the modern Akan and has shown that the period between A.D. 1300 and 1800 constituted a major formative era in the arts of the Akan.

The African, it has been observed by the well-known musicologist, Kwabena Nketia, is born, named, initiated into manhood, warriored, armed, housed, betrothed, wedded, and buried to music. This is generally true of the past and modern Akan and is confirmed in the works of a number of European writers. For instance, 17th-century authors such as Pieter de Marees and Jean Barbot described and illustrated the varied cultural elements of Fanteland including the splendid state drums decorated with relief designs and ivory side-blown trumpets. Bosman, writing in 1704 (*A New and Accurate Description of the Coast of Guinea*, London, 1705, p. 139), described the drum, horn, and iron castanet ensembles of the Akan and remarked that the combination of these instruments produced 'the most charming music that can be imagined'. In 1817, Bowdich, thoroughly overwhelmed by the magnificent welcome ceremony accorded him at Kumase, wrote:

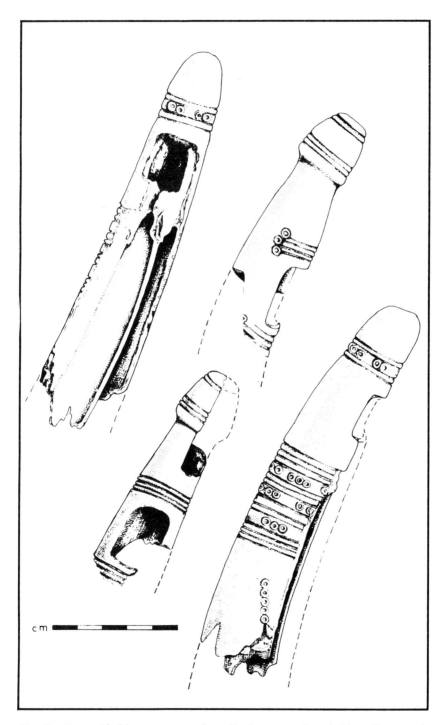

cm

Fig. 8.7 Ivory side-blown trumpets from Begho excavations (16th–17th century)

More than a hundred bands burst forth at once on our arrival with the peculiar airs of their several chiefs; the horns flourished their defiances with the beating of innumerable drums and metal instruments and then yielded for a while to the soft breathings of their long flutes which were truly harmonious and a pleasing instrument like a bagpipe was happily blended.

(*Mission from Cape Coast to Ashantee*, London, 1819, p. 34)

Bowdich made a survey of 19th-century Asante musicians and their instruments – fiddles, calabash rattles, *odurugya* flutes for playing funeral dirges, *Atenteben* flutes, and the ivory horns used at state ceremonies, the *Seperewa*, the iron gongs, iron castanets, and a variety of Akan drums. He was struck by the way the locals could communicate in surrogate or symbolic language by means of drums and noted that 'an old resident has assured me he has heard these flute dialogues and that every sentence was explained to him'. Dupuis, who visited Kumase shortly after Bowdich, gave a striking example of Akan surrogate communication in his recording of the praise songs of the Asante court herald who chanted the praises of the Asante chief, Opoku Kojo:

Where shall we find such a warrior as the strong and beautiful Opoku Kojo
Whose eyes are like the panther in fight?
O great slave of the king.
how you are beloved!
Your victories delight his ears
who fought the Gyamans and killed their leader Adovai?
Opoku Kojo?
Where are the women, and the gold?
Opoku Kojo has them.
He is a rich man; a mighty man.
His enemies die when he is angry.
He is invulnerable
(*Journal of a Residence in Ashantee*, London, 1824, p. 78)

Akan archaeo-musicology is limited to the study of actual musical instruments or their artistic representations found in ancient Akan sites. For instance, the Begho excavations unearthed actual ivory side-blown trumpets used by the Brong Akan of the area for court music-making around the 16th century (Fig. 8.7). The excavation of a 17th-century mausoleum at Adanse Ahinsan revealed clay sculptures of trumpets and of court trumpeters as well as gongs represented in high relief on funerary sculpture (Fig. 8.8). Another archaeological investigation at Twifo Hemang on a 17th-century Assin funerary site revealed what appear to be royal burials with clay sculptures of 'talking drums'.

The early history of the Akan is partly written in pottery. Pottery is the artefact with the greatest potential for survival. Pottery styles easily betray their cultural bearers. Pottery can be traded over wide areas. Thus pottery enables the archaeologist to trace the origins, movements, cultural evolution and trade relations of different ethnic groups. It is not yet possible to pin-point with certainty the beginnings of Akan pottery technology. But the earliest-known pottery which oral traditions associate with an Akan ethnic group is that recorded recently in the Nyarko suburb of Begho, dated by radiocarbon to around the 11th century. The Nyarko potters made quite elegant bowls and jars coated with slip and polychrome painting, sometimes in geometrical design. This ceramic tradition which is rare in Ghana south of latitude 8° north has its homeland in the Sahel and Sudan belts stretching from Dakar across to Tchad.

Ethno-linguistic evidence in the northern Akan area indicates that in the past there have been small movements into the area by people with Sudanic traits. The early Begho painted pottery tradition may therefore be a reflection of this cultural or human contact between the two areas. More characteristic of Akan pottery is the technique of producing a bright, lustrous decorative effect on pottery by means of 'smoke glazing' or pottery dyeing. This ceramic style is recorded in ruins of many Akan villages and towns of the last 500 years, but the best examples found so far are from 17th-century Ahinsan. This same period saw considerable diversification of pottery styles, indicative both of a proliferation of specialist potters and general cultural diversification. The earlier, simpler forms of Akan pottery were transformed during the era of political and economic expansion into elaborate polymorphic forms such as pedestalled, quinlobate, zoomorphic and multi-handled types. Low-relief and high-relief designs which appear in contemporary local metal vessels were beautifully worked in the clay medium – bosses, ridges, tassels, as well as solar, floral and animal motifs.

The Akan are well-known for their art in the media of wood, brass, copper, textiles and clay. Their skills of wood-carving of stools and drums were already known when the earliest Portuguese made contact with Elmina and other Fante groups. Oral traditions trace the use of the wooden stool or *asesedwa* as a symbol of office back to the pre-European period in Adanse and Brong Ahafo. These stools not only reflected the status of their owners but also inculcated artistic symbols

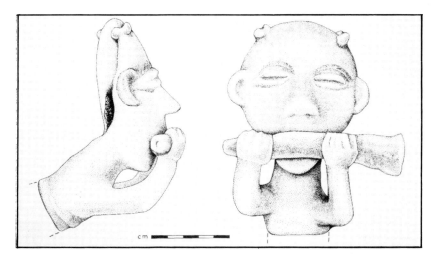

Fig. 8.8 16th/17th century clay sculpture of a court trumpeter from excavations at Ahinsan (Asante)

which were of religious, philosophical and cultural significance. So far, no wooden stools have been found in archaeological contexts. The oldest preserved Akan royal wooden stools include the 17th-century stool of the Denkyira King Ntim Gyakari. This stool is now in the museum of Akan culture at Kumasi. One of the media in which the ancient Akan demonstrated their remarkable art and craft skills was in brass technology. The numerous brass weights for weighing gold executed in the past few centuries by the *cire perdue* method in geometrical and figurative shapes, and are now found in many museums and private collections all over the world, are indicative of the measure of the Akan achievement in this craft. The oldest-known Akan symbolic brass weights belong to the 17th century and are in the form of cast animal figures. Probably, the most intriguing brass sculptures found in an Akan state are two lamps which are alleged to have been discovered in graves at Atebubu. Anthony Arkell has suggested that they are local imitations of Egyptian Byzantine lamps. Most of the extant examples of the magnificent gold sculptures and masks of the Akan are not older than the 19th century.

Akan clay sculpture has evinced greater power of survival in archaeological deposits. It thus provides us with a good deal of detail for historical and cultural reconstruction. Archaeological research at Beifikrom in Fanteland and Twindorasi in Kwahuland, where cultural material not associated with European imports or local smoking pipes has been unearthed, suggests that the Akan practice of making disc-shaped terracotta heads resembling in form the modern *akuaba* fertility dolls began in the pre-European period. Sometime in the 17th century, this evolved into three-dimensional sculpture which was conceived not so much as art for art's sake but as cultural material to serve as part of the equipment or furniture at funeral ceremonies. According to traditional accounts, recorded by the anthropologist, R. S. Rattray, on the sixth day after a person's death, relatives shaved their hair and clipped their finger nails and put them in a clan pot which they deposited near the grave together with sculptured portraits of the deceased and pots containing mashed yam, palm soup and palm wine. Some of the clan pots have high relief or low relief epitaph art work which seems to depict the activities and achievements of the deceased in his or her lifetime, or serves as a form of proverbial pictographic script embodying philosophical and religious statements intended to console the soul of the dead person and his or her living relatives. Rattray's information is confirmed by oral traditions narrated to R. B. Nunoo in the 1950s by a famous potter and clay sculptor, Madam Abena Owu (1866–1956) who used to supply figurines to royal houses in Agona, Akyem and Asante. Nunoo writes in the *Proceedings of the 7th Pan-African Congress of Prehistory* (Addis Ababa, 1976, p. 311):

> According to this specialist, after completing an order, libation is poured with a brief prayer that the figures may truly represent those whose image appeared in water at the commencement of the work. At the same time, the spirit of the deceased is invoked into the figures before they are handed over to the customers who take them to the cemetery and perform almost identical ceremony there.

In 1602 Pieter de Marees described Elmina funerary customs and ceremonies associated with the manufacture of clay portraits and clan pots:

All kinds of food and drink are put on the grave in order that they

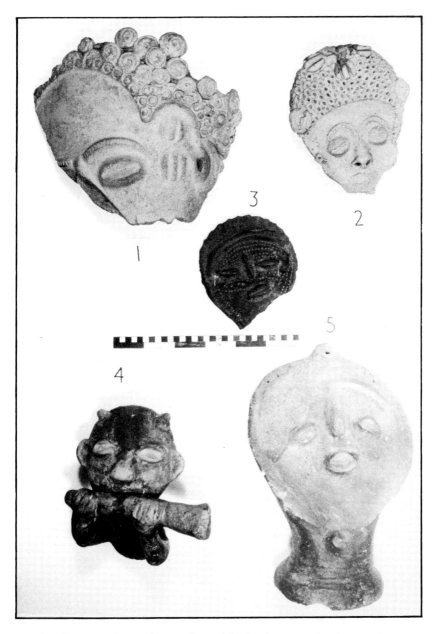

Fig. 8.9 Funerary clay sculptures from Akanland: 1, 2 and 4 from 17th-century Ahinsan, 3 from 17th-century Abiriw, Akwapem; 5 from 16th-century Kwahu

may eat them, and they believe also in good faith that they actually consume this food and drink and live on it, and the pots with water and palm wine are constantly renewed. All his baggage, such as his weapons and his clothes, are buried with him, and all his nobles who served him (during his life time) are imitated in earth from the life and painted and put in a row all round the grave, one next to the other so that their sepulchres are like a house and furnished in a manner as if they were still alive.

(P. de Marees, *A Description and Historical Declaration of the Golden Kingdom of Guinea*, Glasgow, 1604, p. 191)

Examples of funerary sculpture depicting human heads, or illustrating objects used at Akan political and social functions such as court

Fig. 8.10 Funerary clay sculpture of a king from Enchi

regalia, trumpets, drums, state swords, sandals, and caskets for storing jewellery have been found in excavations in 17th-century mausolea at Assin Twifo and at Ahinsan and Fomena in Asante. Surface collections from Agoɐa Swedru, Asebu and Kwahu and fifteen sites located within a 50-kilometres radius of Enchi in southwestern Ghana, all suggest that this was a general Akan custom (Figs. 8.9, 8.10, 8.11). Some Ahinsan funerary sculpture depicting women carrying water-pots on their heads seems symbolic of belief in a perpetuation of earthly life hereafter, where the same servants would serve the deceased, a philosophy which is still strongly held today among some Akan groups. Akan funerary art represented in clan pots has ethnographic parallels in modern clan pots, diverse crafts, traditional cult shrines and royal residences in Asante, Kwahu, Cape Coast and Biriwa. The 17th-century examples of Twifo Hemang and Adanse are already full-blown and we do not as yet have evidence of their earliest antecedents which may date to between A.D.

Fig. 8.11 Funerary clay sculpture from Enchi

1300 and 1500, because the wooden stool, the drum and ivory trumpet and the gong around which Akan symbolism and symbolic language evolved were already well-established in Akan court regalia at the time of the earliest European visitors (Fig. 8.12). It appears from the contemporary evidence that there was cultural continuity so that we find some of the 17th-century Akan symbolism exactly paralleled in modern symbols which represent well-known proverbs. William Abraham, writing in his book, *The Mind of Africa* (p. 111), states: 'Akan philosophy was not scholastic; it receded into the village and was related to religion, law and traditional art.' The ancient Akan used their arts and crafts as a medium for expressing their deepest philosophical and religious thinking. In keeping with the Akan proverb *'oba nyansafo yebu no be yenka no asem'* (an intelligent person is admonished in proverbs not in pedestrian language), these profound thoughts were conveyed not in everyday language but in proverbs, the philosopher's language.

A few examples of Akan pictographic writing found on clan pots and domestic pots in Late Iron Age mausolea at Ahinsan, Fomena and Twifo Hemang may be cited here. The ladder symbolises the proverb, *'owu atwede obakofo mfro'* – it is the destiny of every man to descend the ladder of death (Fig. 8.13). The shield symbolises the proverb, *'ekyem tete a eka ne mrebo'* – when the shield of life disintegrates its framework survives, meaning, a man's achievements are immortal (Fig. 8.13, middle). The knobbed St. Andrew's cross symbolises a proverb on the immortality of the soul – 'Onyame bewu na mewu' (If God could die, so would I) (Fig. 8.14). The outstretched dead frog symbolises the sarcastic proverb *'eda aponkyirenibewu na yebehu netenten'* – the frog's real measure and worth is known only after his death.

The ancient Akan believed in *Onyame*, the Supreme Being and Creator of all things and they had special temples, altars, and priests

Fig. 8.12 17th-century Ahinsan clan pot with gong and manillas in high relief

dedicated to *Onyame*. In a typical Akan family house was kept the *Nyame dua*, the altar of the sky-god. This altar comprised a forked post topped by a brass or clay vessel filled with herbs and water regularly sprinkled on the domestic inmates for spiritual protection. *The Nyame dua* symbol depicting a person making an offering to *Onyame*, was often employed in the casting of gold weights for which there is ethnographic evidence. Parallel to Akan monotheism there was a cult of lesser gods connected with several deities and the use of charms.

Among the Brong of Bono Manso, Takyiman, Nsawkaw and Wenchi there are still extant ancient temples dedicated to the lesser deities, such as Ntoa, Tano, Takwesi, Takofi, Takwabena. Some of the shrines at Nsawkaw, the direct successor state of ancient Begho, and also at Bono Manso have brass bowls filled with ritual objects and sacred water. A few of the brass bowls at Nsawkaw have Arabic inscriptions dated to the 14th and 15th century which provide a clue to the chronology of the development of state formation and organized traditional religion in the area provided that there is not too long a gap

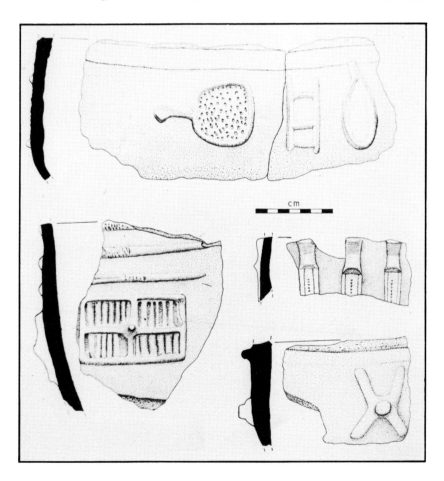

Fig. 8.13 17th-century Ahinsan clan pots with symbolic pictographs

between the making of the vessel, its importation, and its adoption as a sacred shrine vessel.

Reference has already been made to the indigenous religious architecture of Adanse (chapter 3), examples of some of which are still extant and are descendants of types constructed in the late 17th century at the inception of the Asante kingdom. Adanse architectural symbolic art (Fig. 3.2), like the funerary pottery art, is in effect a pictographic form of writing, one aspect of Akan civilization which reached its peak in 19th-century Asante. Like the language of the Akan iron gong, the *fontomfrom* drum, the wooden stool and the *adowa* dance, the pictographs of Adanse architecture are but a short step away from ideographic, sound or alphabetical writing. It is known that in Bronze Age Egypt and Mesopotamia, there was little distinction made between the scribe who expressed himself in words and the artist who embodied his ideas in form. Indeed, one of the might-have-beens of African history is that if the introduction of European and Arabic language and script into Ghana had been delayed, the Akan may well have evolved by now their own indigenous script.

In 1817, T. E. Bowdich led a British government mission to Kumase, the Asante capital. Among other things, the mission was required 'to report fully their opinion of the inhabitants and of the progress they have made in the arts of civilised life'. The report of the

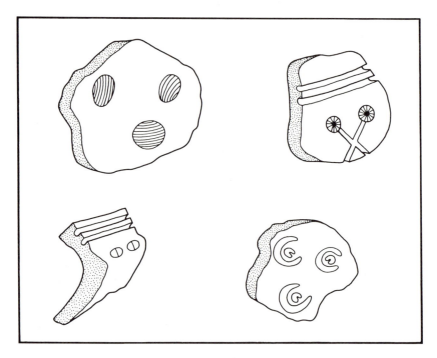

Fig. 8.14 Fragments of clan pots with symbolic pictographs from excavations at Twifo Hemang 16th/17th century mausolea (Assin), after J. Bellis, 'Ceramic analysis and the construction of chronological sequences at Twifo Heman', West African Journal of Archaeology, 1976, p. 75

mission which was published by Bowdich in 1819 gave a vivid description of early 19th-century Asante life as well as notes on Asante history since A.D. 1700. Bowdich was very much impressed by what he saw. He noted the following facts:

> that the Asante political system was highly organised and headed by an astute king, Osei Tutu Kwamina, whose sense of justice and liberality 'would have ennobled the most civilized monarch' and that a state council with ministers and a civil service and an army of over 20 000 provided enforcement to government policies, that at its height, Asante empire covered territorially nearly the whole of present-day Ghana; that it had large towns and its capital, Kumasi, was a 'city', eight kilometres in circumference, with a population of between 12 000 and 15 000, suburbs and ornate storied buildings; that Asante had a diversified technological system including iron metallurgy, gold and silver smithing, and elaborate centralized craft work in textiles, ivory, beads, wooden stools, and pottery; that the buoyant and diverse economy of the kingdom based on plantation agriculture and commerce in kola, ivory, and gold, involved considerable organisation of markets, the opening, maintenance and policing of trade routes and the use of currency such as gold dust; that the social structure comprised a principal Akan core, and a small group of immigrant traders and settlers from northern Ghana, northern Nigeria and Mali; that most Asante people practised in traditional monumental architecture the ancestral traditional religion which inculcated both monotheistic and polytheistic ideas and which ran through the entire fabric of society; that Islam had since the mid-18th century made some headway in Asante manifesting itself in Asante *Kramo* community with muslim chaplains, mosque architecture, and Koranic teachers and schools; that Asante social festivals, royal durbars and state ceremonies were invariably graced by the display of Asante's unique traditional crafts and colourful regalia, accompanied by well-developed music and dance expressing the most profound surrogate language which Bowdich described as 'magnificent and enchanting'.
> (Bowdich, *Mission from Cape Coast Castle to Ashantee*, London, 1819).

The recent work of John Fynn, *Asante and her Neighbours*, and that of Ivor Wilks, *Asante in the 19th Century*, more than substantiate the views of Bowdich. However, Bowdich did not realise that the Asante already had a rudimentary traditional literate culture expressed in pictographs, rich in philosophical ideas and manifested not just among the upper class or in the civil service, but in the cultural materials of everyday life, on pottery, textiles, metal work, drums, religious temples, in music and dance and in folk stories and proverbs.

In archaeology and anthropology the term 'civilization' is used, not ethically or subjectively, but rather to represent a definite stage in the development of human society and culture. Civilization involves the creation of a complex artificial environment characterised by such traits as large towns or cities, complex agricultural and industrial installations, trade, architecture and art, science, literacy, and complex social and political systems. By any standards and criteria, the Asante kingdom, whose foundations were laid in Middle Iron Age Adanse, evolved from the end of the 17th century what was clearly an indigenous civilization although it received influences from external sources. Asante was the apogee of Akan cultural development, although chronologically late as compared to the early civilizations of the Old World and New World, such as Sumeria, Pharaonic Egypt, Kush, Indus, Shang China, Minoan-Mycenae and Meso-America. But when all the criteria of civilization have been considered – language and communication, technology, art, architecture, political, economic and social organisation and ideological developments – it can be said that the available evidence, however fragmentary or circumstantial, does suggest that the Akan sometime between A.D. 1000 and 1700 progressed rapidly from the level of peasant agricultural communities to the level of urban societies and principalities, culminating in the establishment of an indigenous civilization.

9 The Accra plains – civilization of the Ga-Dangme

The Accra coastlands are today inhabited by the Ga-Dangme peoples. The Dangme occupy the eastern part while the Ga are located in the west. The modern Dangme comprise the people of Shai, La, Ningo, Kpone, Osudoku, Gbugbla, Krobo and Ada who speak different dialects of the Dangme language. The modern Ga comprise, firstly, the Ga Mashie who occupy Asere, Gbese, and Sempe in the central part of Accra, and secondly, other Ga-speakers who migrated from places such as Fanteland, Akwapem, Akwamu, La, Aneho (in Togo) and Lagos (Nigeria) to live in the areas of Osu, Labadi, Teshi, Tema, Nungua, and Korle Gonno. The Ga and Dangme have some similarities in language, social and political institutions and certain cultural features.

Ga-Dangme origins

The problem of the origins of the Ga-Dangme is still unresolved after decades of research by linguists, historians and archaeologists. The old view which still persists in oral traditions is that the Ga-Dangme migrated into Ghana from external sources of origin. Oral traditions documented by the author in a number of Ga and Dangme towns suggest that the Ga-Dangme came from somewhere east of the Accra plains. Places mentioned include Togo, Dahomey and Yorubaland. However, the Ga who have a *kple* song in which they state that '*wo dzee he dzeke*', meaning, 'we migrated from a very distant country', state in their oral traditions that their migration from the Togo–Dahomey–Yorubaland areas followed an earlier stage in their long migration which originally commenced somewhere in Egypt, Babylonia and Levant or Mesopotamia. Neither the Dangme as a group nor the Ga as a group had a consensus on the question of origins. There appears to be a tendency for individual local towns and villages or clan groups to want to gain some prestige by attributing to themselves origins from famous ancient civilizations in Egypt, Israel, North Africa, or Nigeria. For instance, recently, the author was told by the chief of Ayawaso, old capital of 17th-century Great Accra, that the Ga originally came from the land of Canaan under the leadership of the biblical Joshua and sojourned in savanna country in West Africa before coming to settle finally in the Nsaki valley at Ayawaso. The chief of Shai at Doryumu, successor state of 17th-century Shai, informed the author that the Dangme migrated to the Accra plains from southern Nigeria, while the chief of Gbugbla (Prampram) referred to Tetetutu in the Dahomey-Togo area as the original homeland of the Dangme. Some linguists have taken the traditions at their face value and sought to use certain language similarities to link the Ga-Dangme with certain peoples in the Togo–Dahomey–Nigeria area and so given their support to the view of external origins. But the historian, Adu Boahen, has argued in the *Ghana Social Science Journal* (1977, p. 94) that:

> The Ewe speak a language closely related to the Fon and Adja languages spoken in Togo and Dahomey while the Ga and Adangbe and the Krobo speak virtually the same language. Not only are these four languages quite distinctive, and not only are all of them spoken in clearly defined and continuous areas; but with the exception of Ewe, all the other languages are spoken here in Ghana and nowhere else in the world. It was therefore here in Ghana that these languages evolved and nowhere else, and since it takes at least a thousand years for a language to break off from a parent language or a proto-language and develop into a language of its own, it follows that at least some of the speakers of these languages must have been living in these regions for at least a thousand years.

Boahen cites accounts of Eustace De La Fosse, who was on the coast of Ghana in 1479, and Pacheco Pereira, who was in Ghana in the 1500s, as indicating that there was a maritime trade in slaves, cloth and beads organized by the Portuguese between the Nigerian coast and Elmina in the late 15th and early 16th centuries; that this trade was

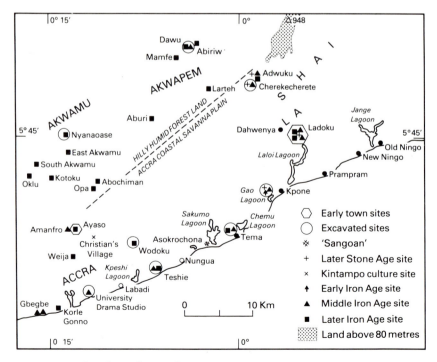

Map 9.1 Archaeological sites of Accra area

probably pre-European in origin; and that the traditions of the Ga-Dangme that they migrated from the Nigeria area may simply be distortions down the centuries of these pre-Portuguese trading connections.

There is as yet no shred of archaeological evidence to confirm the view of external origin of the Ga-Dangme. The weakness of archaeology is that artefacts cannot by themselves speak out, except figuratively, to attest to the ethnic identity of their makers. However, when oral traditions related to the distribution patterns of present and past populations are correlated with historical linguistics and archaeological distributions of sites and their cultural contents, it is possible to glean some facts about the origins of people and their cultural development. Recent archaeological studies (Map 9.1) aided by the application of radiocarbon dating suggest that the Accra plains were inhabited during the first four millennia B.C. by Late Stone Age hunter-gatherers who were also given to fishing for fresh water molluscs. Their quartz stone flake and microlithic industries have been found in excavations at Legon, Gao Lagoon, and Ladoku and in surface reconnaissance in the hills of Shai and Cherekecherete and in the areas of Accra airport, Kaneshie and Weija. The final stages of the Late Stone Age witnessed the establishment of village settlements which made pottery ornamented by stamping. Examples of this pottery have been excavated at Gao lagoon site where they were found with large quantities of remains of shell fish. Stamped pottery associated with quartz flakes were excavated from the lowest level at Ladoku hill, located a few kilometres north of Gao lagoon. Cigar-shaped palettes were found together with stamped pottery in the ruins of Late Stone Age village settlements at Christian's village close to the campus of Legon University (Fig. 2.1). A number of radiocarbon dates obtained from recent excavations in the Kpone and Ladoku area of the eastern Accra plains suggest that during the Early and Middle Iron Age, especially between A.D. 500 and 1400, there was an expansion of village settlements. Surface reconnaissance at Weija and Gbegbe and excavations at the University Drama Studio site have shown that there were similar events in the western and central Accra plains. By the end of the Middle Iron Age, there were numerous villages of various sizes located along the beaches of the Accra plains and along inland streams and rivers such as the Ohudaw, Dechidaw, Padinyegbete, Nsaki and Densu. These communities knew iron working, exploited local clay resources for the manufacture of pottery which was profusely decorated with comb stamp and roulette impressions, grooves and high relief patterns, and continued the Late Stone Age tradition of shell fish subsistence economy. Their pottery, which was marketed widely in the Accra plains, is distinct from the more sophisticated pottery of the Late Iron Age. The archaeological sites which produce Middle Iron Age wares in eastern Accra are located in areas which oral traditions and present-day ethnic distributions associate mainly with the Dangme, who have an extant tradition of potting which may extend for a millennium into the past. Those sites which produce Middle Iron Age wares in the central and western Accra plains are located in areas which oral traditions and present-day ethnic distributions associate mainly with the Ga Mashie or nuclear Ga.

The rise of towns and kingdoms

The radiocarbon evidence suggests that by the 14th century, the eastern Accra plain cultural complex was flourishing on specialist activities including potting, fish-processing and probably salt-making and commerce based on these industries. On a hill called Cherekecherete in Shai, which has excellent clay deposits and is littered with thousands of potsherds now designated Cherekecherete ware, there are stone enclosures and what appear to be stone agricultural terraces. The ruins of similar structures have been found at Ladoku where Cherekecherete ware has been discovered in excavations at the northern and southern ends of a settlement which extended over an area roughly two kilometres by one kilometre. At Ladoku hill, the finest Cherekecherete pottery with elegant artistic motifs of bosses and what appear to be stylized cattle, goat or human female heads, was found in association with a bauxite and quartz bead industry and with shell fish remains (Fig. 9.1). Cherekecherete ware has been found at Kpone, Tema, Adwuku and the University Drama Studio site. On the grounds of territorial extent, an estimated population size of about 4 000 and the probable existence of a combination of primary and secondary economic activities, it may be suggested that the site of Ladoku was in the 14th century either a town or was on the way to becoming one. Dangme traditions state that this was the residence of the Dangme dynasty whose founder, called La Nimo, first established the nuclear Dangme settlement in the Lolovo hills of Tagalogo near Osudoku. If this is so, it suggests that state formation in the eastern Accra plains may have begun sometime in the 13th century.

The laying of the foundation of towns and states in Galand would appear to have slightly post-dated and perhaps even taken its cue from the Dangme example, though this statement needs confirmation from further archaeological and historical study. According to Ga traditions, in the 15th century, a resourceful priest-ruler of Asere, one of the Ga

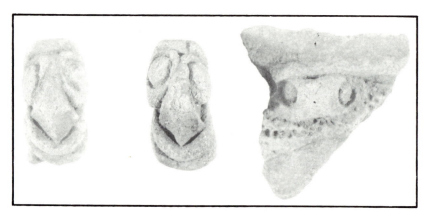

Fig. 9.1 Animal figurines attached to 14th/15th century Cherekecherete ware (Accra plains)

nuclear settlements in the central Accra area, succeeded in amalgamating some thirty Ga settlements into a centralized kingdom under his rule. When, in the middle of the 16th century, the Portuguese initiated the European maritime trade along the Accra coastlands, according to oral traditions the Ga were mining alluvial gold from the Nsaki-Densu basins for sale to the Portuguese. With the increasing demand for more and better-quality gold, king Ayite of the Asere dynasty chose Ayawaso, traditionally one of the Ga nuclear settlements, as the new Ga capital site, on account of Ayawaso location closer to the gold-producing regions of the southern Akan. In 1962, following research at Ayawaso, the archaeologist Paul Ozanne wrote in the *Transactions of the Historical Society of Ghana*:

> Here (at Ayaso), middens mark the site of a large town, extending for a mile along the southern bank of the small river Nsachi and across the stream to the modern village of Amanfro; and the surface scatter of pottery and iron slag covers a much larger area. The ruins of the town have been intensively farmed and most of the details of its plan have been obliterated; the middens have been spread out to merge into one another, and many small piles of stone beside the farmers' plots suggest that a number of stone house-foundations have been destroyed. Ayaso is traditionally remembered as the site of an early town of the Ga Mashi and Awutu (Obutu).

With the advent of European traders, there was a change in the economy of the settlements of the Accra plains. The Portuguese began their commercial activities in the Accra area around 1550. In 1557, the English trader, Towerson, bought gold from Accra. The Portuguese, fearing English and other European competition, were quick to erect a trade fort on the coast of Accra but it was short-lived, as the local people soon attacked the fort and razed it to the ground. Nevertheless, Portuguese imported cloth, brass basins, manillas, iron rods, and sugar was probably introduced into the Accra plains at this time. The Dutchman, Pieter de Marees, who visited the country in 1601, referred to 16th-century Portuguese enterprise in Accra. The 17th century was a boom period in Ga commerce with the Dutch, English, Swedes, Danes, and French. This led to the erection of three European forts, namely, the Dutch fort Crevecoeur in 1642, the Danish fort, Christiansborg, in 1661, and the English fort, James, in 1672. The Ga bought gold, slaves and ivory from the inland peoples and sold to the Europeans in exchange for firearms, textiles, metal work and alcohol. Some of these foreign goods and Ga-produced fish, salt and corn were sold by the Asere traders at Ayawaso in exchange for foodstuffs and livestock obtained from hinterland peoples.

By the 17th century, Accra had become celebrated for its maritime commerce, especially in gold. Van den Broecke, writing in the early 17th century, said of Accra: 'to this place comes down indeed the most and best gold of this whole coast'. Tilleman described the trade of Ayawaso in the late 17th century. Olfert Dapper observed that small Accra was a centre of attraction for European merchants bringing iron, linen and other goods in exchange for gold. The Huguenot, Jean Barbot, described Accra as 'that golden country' whose people furnished the Danes, Dutch and English with more gold and slaves than did the whole Gold Coast. Barbot noted that the Akyem sold at Nungua port prisoners taken from their wars at Akwamu, while the latter sold their prisoners at Accra port; that in return the Europeans sold cowries, textiles, iron knives, guns and gunpowder to the Accra people; and that but for the constant Akwamu–Akyem conflicts, the trade of Accra could have been far greater. The Ga became the entrepreneurs for the European trade and a new class of artisans, interpreters, canoe-men and brokers soon emerged along the coast. At Abonse, described by the 1629 Dutch map-maker of Moure as 'A.B.C.' a great market and entrepot grew up a few kilometres north of Ayawaso. Here, inland traders came to sell their goods in exchange for European manufactured goods. This middleman enterprise brought the Ga considerable profit and increased the power and prestige of their kingdom. The Ga state army made up of 15 000 people armed with guns, spears and swords was the object of discussion by Dapper and Roemer.

The Dangme peoples of the eastern Accra plains had commercial relations with the European nations though this took a less spectacular turn than that of the Ga. Barbot referred to the late 16th and early 17th century towns of Ladingcour (Ladoku) and Prampram and their commercial activities.

The Dutch went on Bosman's record in 1704 as having erected a trade post at Kpone by 1700, and the Danes built a fort there in the early 18th century. At about the same time, the English built a trade post at Ningo and from 1730, the Danes followed it up with a number of forts at Ningo and other sites along the coast of east Accra.

The archaeology of Ga-Dangme land confirms the evidence of European written records and provides details related to the inception and expansion of commerce between the Ga-Dangme and the European nations during the two centuries 1550 to 1750. The author's excavations in 1976–79 at the Dangme capital of La and the Ga inland capital of Great Accra at Ayawaso provide some insight into the nature of the Ga and Dangme kingdoms during the early period of European contact. Both at La and Ayawaso an old rubbish dump was excavated. The advantage of excavating a litter site is that it provides a quick cross-sectional picture of most of the technological, economic and other cultural activities of a community. At Ladoku hill, a circular incinerator built of mud (Fig. 1.2 and 1.5) was found to contain products of local activities. These included pottery, iron work, brass work, smoking pipes, fragments of remains of wattle-and-daub and stone houses, nearly 2 000 shells of fresh water molluscs, a large quantity of bones of cattle, sheep, goats and pigs, together with a few of their horn cores, and some thirty sets of granite and quartz stone querns and grinders used in the preparation of food (Fig. 1.3). The pottery quality represents the high-water mark of potting craft attained by the Dangme of Shai, the most likely source of La pottery during this period. There is a diversification of pottery forms and decorative styles which distinguishes the 16th- and 17th-century ceramics from those of the Middle Iron Age of the same area. The Ladoku excavation produced a variety of pot-forms including handled jars, large water pots, and food bowls characterised by cylindrical pedestals with everted foot-rings (Fig. 9.2). Much of this pottery is decorated with a variety of incised, comb stamped or roulette impressions. But the distinctive styles which make a break with the past are the new surface treatments such as coating with red haematite and 'smoke glazing', achieved either by smoking the red-hot pottery in burning leaves or by impregnating the red-hot fired pottery in a coloured dye-liquid. Locally-made smoking pipes were found with this type of pottery. These locally-made artefacts occurred in association with 17th-century Rhenish imported pottery and other European imported pottery, fragments of clay pipes made in Holland and England in the 17th and early 18th centuries, imported beads including 17th century rosetta cane beads from Venice and a large number of cowries of *Cypraea moneta* or *Cypraea annulus* species, known to have been imported from the Maldives, Taheita, Japan or the Indian and Pacific Ocean islands.

Examples of most of these local and imported artefacts found in the incinerator of Ladoku hill were also found in test excavations in the central and southern parts of Ladoku. Detailed surface reconnaissance of the Shai hills have shown that another 16th- and 17th-century Dangme town located there had a similar material culture as Ladoku and was also closely involved in the coastal European trade. Some of the Shai and Ladoku pottery, especially the black lustrous ware decorated with incised solar motifs and tassel reliefs, is exactly paralleled in the

Fig. 9.2 Pottery from 17th-century levels at Ladoku

17th-century midden site of Dawu in Akwapem excavated by Thurstan Shaw. This argues trade not only between the Dangme settlements of Shai and La but also between the Dangme settlements and the Akan and Guan settlements of the Akwapem hills and it also accounts for European imports found in the Dawu mound. Local Dangme traditions have it that the market of old La was noted for its cotton which was popular with the Ga, Dangme and Akwamu settlements of the 16th and 17th century which normally used bark cloth. As no evidence of local cotton cloth industries has so far been found in archaeological excavations in Dangmeland during the last two decades, it must be concluded provisionally that the old La cloths were probably imported from Europe and put on sale in the town, hence the La saying, '*Ke iye la o, mawo tsobo*', meaning, 'Unless I go to La, I can only make do with bark cloth'. Although there continued to be a trading settlement at old La after 1620 for which there is substantial archaeological evidence, it is clear that the main township came to an end sometime around that date. The anonymous Dutch map of 1629 locates Labadi as a coastal settlement between Ga Mashi and Nungua. According to Labadi oral traditions, the people of Labadi were formerly Dangme people who lived near Dawhenya, the site now called Ladoku or derelict La, but that they left Dangmeland after a civil war and moved to Adjangote before settling finally in their present site close to the Atlantic Ocean. A literate chieftain of Shai, Nene Matey Gromodji, recounted in 1978 the oral history related to the fall of old La township:

> At the time when my ancestors first began trading with the Europeans, the Dangme of Shai, La and Ningo had one language, one government, one law, and one culture. At the time, the Dangme chief called La Nimo promulgated a law forbidding males of Shai and La from indulging in illicit sex relations with women from each other's towns. The law made this crime punishable by execution. Shortly afterward, a man from La town seduced a woman from the Hiowe clan of Shai and he was executed. Next, the son of the Shai chief, Prince Adzate was caught in the act with Ometse, wife of the La sub-chief called Odoi. But the Shai chief refused to give up Adzate for execution. This led to war between the two leading Dangme towns – Shai and La. The La war-chief, Sodze and his army were defeated and the La abandoned their town for Adjangote. Meanwhile, the La Army General, Sodze, formed a military alliance with Akwamu, invaded Shai and smote the Shai people hip and thigh so they were compelled to migrate to Tabligbo.

The La-Shai civil war is still commemorated in a traditional Dangme song which the author recorded among the Gbugbla people at Dawhenya:

> *Ometse yoo he ne ta ba nge La ne,*
> *Ao, Ometse, Ao Ometse yoo he ne ta ba nge La ne.*
> Alas, alas, for the Ometse woman
> That she was the cause of war at La,
> Alas, the Ometse women, alas, alas.

Other versions of the cause of the La-Shai civil war were recorded at Dawhenya and Prampram to the effect that the La people held an annual traditional festival to their god, La Kpa, accompanied by singing and an infamous sexual dance. On one occasion, the queen of Shai attended the La Kpa dance and was accosted by the La male dancers. The Shai chief was furious about this, declared war on La and defeated them. Today, the site of old La is indeed deserted as the name Ladoku suggests, except for the occasional Gbugbla inhabitant of nearby Dawhenya town who visits the site either to farm, quarry stone or to fetch fire-wood. The site is remarkable for its large number of baobab trees, *Adansonia digitata*, of which about two hundred can be counted from the air photograph. Some of the largest baobabs may date to the final phase of the old La settlement. The baobab is known to be an all-purpose tree. Local traditions state that its leaves served as vegetables for stews and soups; its fruit contained juice for making porridge; its roots were used for medicinal purposes; its branches provided raw material for making strings; and its main trunk, on account of its lightness, was used for boat-building. Among plants which still grow wild in abundance at Ladoku long after the termination of the old settlement is the *Tulinum triangularis*, a vegetable which was probably cultivated by the people of old La.

The modern village of Ayawaso near Pokoase town is the scene of numerous old house-mounds and middens. These ancient remains lie on the east banks of the Nsaki river whose valley provided a link between the old Ga capital and the old Akwapem settlements of Abiriw and Dawu area. From what is known of the traditional history and archaeology of the area, the environment of modern Ayawaso appears to bear close resemblance to that of old Ayawaso. Present-day Ayawaso has tree-savanna vegetation and numerous oil palm and coconut trees and there is suitable plant food for livestock. Though the annual rainfall is meagre, it is adequate for the cultivation of cassava and maize. The baobab tree and the *Tulinum* vegetable plant still flourish at Ayawaso though not in the same large numbers and not as luxuriantly as at Ladoku. The underlying rock material is made up of fine clay deposits which provide good raw material for potting.

The largest of the middens at Ayawaso measures 20 metres across and stands about $2\frac{1}{2}$ metres in height, though levelling by local farmers has probably reduced it from an original height of about 3 metres. The excavation carried out in 1979 threw light on the economic and industrial life of 17th-century Ga-land (Figs. 1.4 and 9.3). Evidence was found of fragments of walls of furnaces used for iron-smelting and smithing activities as well as slag waste-products and the finished products of iron implements. Examples were unearthed of clay crucibles used for melting down imported brassware or copper rods for the manufacture of ornaments such as bracelets and ear rings which were numbered among the discoveries. It appears these artefacts related to metal technology were from the artisans' quarter whence they were dumped at the midden. Large quantities of fresh water molluscs of different species, numerous bones of domesticated cattle, sheep and goats, bones of wild animals and charred remains of kernels of the oil palm *Elaeis guineensis*, all attest to the diversity of the subsistence economy of Great Accra. Two types of pottery were found in the excavation: firstly, an early type, probably made in the 16th century, characterised by a flowing profile, a round base and haematite coating; and secondly a 17th-century type characterised by an angular profile, jars and bowls with cylindrical pedestals and everted foot-rings (Fig. 9.4) and decorated by means of 'smoke glazing' and especially applied high reliefs depicting naturalistic motifs such as plants and snakes. This later pottery type of Great Accra has been found on old Ga settlement sites at Abochiman, Ajenkotoku, Korle Gonno, Oklu, Opa, and Wodoku. The discovery of European imported pottery and beads as well as local smoking pipes in the very top levels of the mound suggest that the contents of the mound may probably date, roughly, to between the middle of the 16th century and the middle of the 17th century. In previous excavations conducted on the southern part of the same mound by the archaeologists Seth Owusu and Paul Ozanne, the dating evidence included trade goods, namely, an

Fig. 9.3 Chief of Ayawaso (Greater Accra) pouring libation to signal the commencement of the 1979 excavations at Ayawaso

early 17th-century Sgraffito plate from Hesse and a mid-17th-century Rhenish blue stone ware. The latter was found in the same level as local smoking pipes shaped like a European briar. This and other evidence from the Accra plains prompted Ozanne to put forward the hypothesis that the manufacture of locally-made smoking pipes did not commence till the European nations began importing tobacco from the New World and that the first local pipes to be made were direct copies of contemporary European imported pipes.

Early Ga-Dangme political and social life

The principal sources of evidence for the reconstruction of the political and social life of the Ga and Dangme peoples are oral traditions, ethnography, and European written records. For, the European traders and visitors did make references to rulers and state elders with whom they came into contact or local military functionaries with whom they crossed swords. Also, in spite of the adoption by the Ga-Dangme of the traits of modern civilization, the framework of traditional political and social structure is still extant and has been examined by anthropologists and ethnographers.

Dangme oral traditions state that the Dangme had nine clans, namely, Asinodze, Blaka, Kpoku, La, Lekpodze, Lenodze, Nangla, Sepote, and Shalom. From the narratives of the La-Shai civil war of the

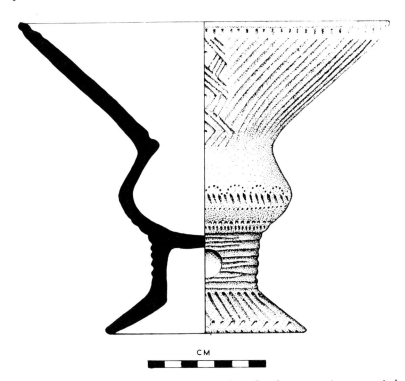

CM

Fig. 9.4 Pedestalled black ware from excavation of 17th-century Ayaso, capital of Great Accra

early 17th century, irrespective of which version of the narratives is right, a number of facts can be inferred: firstly, that the Dangme had a centralized system of government in the past and that this centred around one state ruler; secondly, that the ruler made laws related to matters of social morality and that these were, at least theoretically, applied throughout Dangmeland; that traditional religion took an organized form and was headed by the *Wulomo*, or chief priest, who was at first also the state ruler; and that annual social festivals associated with traditional music and dance were evolved. The narratives also provide hints about the Dangme being organized in six military divisions which did not constitute a standing army but were recruited only in times of war and were led by a war-chief. According to Ga oral traditions, every Ga subject belonged to a family called *We*, and several families constituted a social sector called a quarter or *Akutso*. Each quarter had ruling elders who, together with the king-makers, formed the traditional state council or *Akwashong*, the body that advised the king. The Ga were organized in military divisions in time of war and each division was led by a war-chief.

Oral traditions of both the Dangme and the Ga peoples affirm that their lineage groups were formerly under the political rule of *Wulomei* or high priests who were also custodians of the lineage gods. In this theocracy, the priest was also the secular head. But the exigencies of a society that was becoming increasingly more complex demanded that the priest should delegate his secular duties and powers to two other spiritual colleagues. One became the state guardian, *Mangkralo*, and the other became state father, *Mangtse*. This development appears to have originated among the Dangme of La who moved to the Accra coast in the early 17th century. The story is told that formerly the entire affairs of the La principality were administered by the *Wulomo*, or high priest, of the La Kpa god. Increased secular duties related to politics and trade, land, and warfare during the early period of contact with the European nations led to the separation of the religious and political offices so as to preserve the sacred office of the La Kpa *Wulomo*. Eventually all the towns of the Ga and Dangme adopted this system of government. Since, originally, the rulers of the Ga and Dangme towns were priests, they had no regalia like the Akan royal courts. However, with the settlement among the La of Fanti people from Moure, the creation of the Otublo-him quarter for immigrant Akwamu people, and thanks to the close trade relations between the Ga-Dangme and the Akwapem and Akwamu, Akan socio-political and cultural ideas were introduced into the Ga-Dangme communities. The first chief of Alata, Wetse Kojo, is said to have adopted the Akan *Odwira* festival and also the custom of using an Akan stool as a symbol of office. Eventually nearly all the Ga-Dangme political rulers adopted the Akan stool, state swords and drums, ivory trumpets, the wearing of leather sandals and headgear and the idea of carrying a chief in a palanquin. Not content to borrow cultural materials only, the Ga and Dangme courts adopted the speech-mode of Akan drums and trumpets. What is more, the titles used in Akan traditional system (for instance, *Asafoatse*, head of the war company) and the style of naming of Akan military divisions were adopted and modified for use in Ga-Dangme social context. For instance, the Dangme of Shai were organized in six military divisions under military leaders as follows:

Hiemtatse – Front guard
Hiomitatse – Right Wing
Muomtatse – Left Wing
Mlatsremfotse – Vanguard
Kpetitatse – Commander-in-Chief
Setatse – Rearguard.

J. H. Kwabena Nketia has demonstrated from his study of musical traditions of the Accra coastlands that Ga culture was highly tolerant and adaptive and that the Ga took up the rich cultural traits of the Akan and put them to good use. The songs of certain forms of Ga traditional religion show clear Akan influence:

Awo, awoo aagba ee, bleku tsoo!
Esu esu, enam, enam, manye, o manye a,
Adebani kpotoo!
Exalted, exalted, hark the prophets speak;
Abundant rain, they say, water upon water, fish upon fish,
Peace for peace, and food in abundance.
(M. Kilson, 1971, p. 117)

The Ga are said to have adopted Guan music and religious traits: *Kple*, the Ga cult, employs a mixture of Ga, Obutu (Guan) and Akan vocabulary. But some *Kple* songs such as the following example are thoroughly Akan:

Obi nni Nyampong ase
Obi nni tente woakong
Obi nni dada me wo aye
Obi nni Nyampong ase daa.
No one knows the origin of God,
No one knows the origin of Kple sacred dance,
No one knows the origins of what we do,
No one knows the origins of *Me* which we perform,
No one knows God's origin, ever.
(M. Kilson, 1971, p. 124)

There is evidence, then, of cultural exchange between the Accra coastlands and the neighbouring Akan kingdoms such as Akwapem, Akwamu, Agona, Akyem, and Fante. There is reason to accept oral traditions which say that it was the immigrant Akan who introduced into the Accra region such socio-political traits as the stool, drum, king-carrying in palanquins and Akan song-types each as *Kpanlogo*, *Siolele*, *Adowa*, and *Tumatu*. In fact, traditions are emphatic that the stool is foreign to the Dangme and Ga constitutions and is regarded as an imported fetish. It must be regarded, for better or for worse, as a legacy of the Akan to the evolution of Ga and Dangme political and cultural systems.

10 The legacy of the past

Great states and civilizations hardly ever grow in isolation. They give and take. They make discoveries of their own. They learn and adopt from others. They adapt what is adopted. So it is with Ghana, Ghanaian history and culture. It is like a cloth woven with many multi-coloured threads forming diverse patterns incorporating an older traditional element originating from the indigenous African situation, a Mediterranean and Near Eastern element acquired through the peoples and states of the West African Sudan, and a Western European element which, however belated, has added its own brilliant lustre to the cloth of Ghana. The modern Ghanaian scene is indeed a mosaic of older indigenous systems of rule by chiefs and clan organizations, philosophies, beliefs and practices, languages and literature, music and dance, social festivals and ceremonies, arts and crafts, and methods of subsistence and cash economies side by side with newer forms of foreign government, culture, technology, economic system, language, religion and philosophy adopted from the Western and Islamic worlds. For the cultural historian, it is not an enviable task to set about unravelling this complex cloth of history and culture – warp and woof. It needs the varied professional tools and expertise of the archaeologist, historian, linguist, ethnologist and anthropologist. But thanks to the application of the multi-disciplinary approach to the study of the past, we now have some impression of the general outline of Ghana's past into which the details can be fitted. This outline is admittedly rather faint in its earlier part and a lot clearer in its latter part, but it is nevertheless a useful framework.

In Ghana, only a handful of Stone Age Sites have been excavated. They include the 'Sangoan' and Middle Stone Age industries at Asokrochona and Tema west, the microlithic industries at Bosumpra, Akyekyemabuo, Apreku, Tetewabuo and the Kintampo rockshelters, and a number of 'neolithic' sites. But a substantial amount of surface material has also been collected from all over Ghana. No physical remains of early man have been found. Though organic materials for radiocarbon dating are hard to come by, some Late Stone Age sites have produced shells, charcoal and other materials for dating, for instance, Gao lagoon and the Kwahu rockshelters. These are only a handful of dates. Nevertheless, the handaxes found on the surface of sites and in old river gravels and fossil beaches, the 'Sangoan' and Middle Stone Age picks, choppers, and scrapers found at Asokrochona and elsewhere, the well-attested microlithic industries and the Kintampo culture sites clearly show that Ghana has a fairly long prehistory, probably going back to around 50 000 B.C. at the least, and that the Stone Age bequeathed to Ghana a legacy of human population on which the future population of the country was to be built. This contradicts the oft-held view that the forest land was only recently penetrated by man.

Important technological changes which took place between 10 000 B.C. and 2000 B.C. such as the adoption of the new stone blade technique and the making of polished stone axes, flaked or polished stone arrowheads, bone harpoons and pottery, and the resultant improvement in Stone Age economy paved the way for the introduction of a food production economy into Ghana in the second millennium B.C. It is to these people that later Ghanaians were to be indebted for laying the foundations of food production in the country. Today, the simple methods of wattle-and-daub architecture of Kintampo culture times are still with us, and the polished stone axe, the guide-fossil of the earliest farmers, was to be used in the Iron Age apparently for cultivation, carpentry, and gold mining, not to speak of ritual and medicinal purposes.

It is the Iron Age, however, that we know most about. It is also the period which is of greater relevance to present-day Ghana. As the list of radiocarbon dates in the appendix shows, out of nearly ninety radiocarbon dates obtained so far, two-thirds of that number comprises dates for various stages of Iron Age cultural development. The precise origin of the new technology of this epoch, called Iron Age for want of better expression, as already stated, is still unknown. Recent discoveries in Lake Victoria region have thrown the question even more widely open. P. R. Schmidt, an anthropologist, and D. H. Avery, an engineer, both of them professors at Brown University, U.S.A., recently excavated a large number of iron-smelting furnaces fitted with forced draught blow-pipes at Kemongo Bay on the shores of Lake Victoria, west Tanzania. The sites have been dated to around 500 B.C. Schmidt and Avery wrote (1979):

> We have found a technological process in the African iron age which is exceedingly complex. To be able to say that a technologically superior culture developed in Africa more than 1500 years ago overturns popular and scholarly ideas that technological sophistication developed in Europe but not Africa.

Reluctantly then, we must needs keep an open mind on the matter. But whatever the origins of iron technology, one thing is certain, that the new technology had a profound effect on many aspects of society – agriculture, small-scale industry, mining, trade, defence and territorial expansion – and so aided the emergence of specialists in various fields of society. Until the 1920s, traditional blacksmiths provided the bulk of iron implements and weapons used in northern Ghana, and before the massive importation of iron bars from Europe from A.D. 1500 onwards, middle and southern Ghana relied on local iron workers for the supply of civil and military metal equipment.

We have seen that goldmining was the most outstanding of the indigenous industries which contributed to the rapid development of Ghana in the Iron Age. Attempts made by the Portuguese and the

Dutch at setting up gold mining installations in Ghana after A.D. 1600 proved a fiasco and it was not until the late 19th century that effective European mechanised exploitation of local alluvial and deep mines commenced. Thus the industry which produced all the gold that was traded to Europe and the Islamic world from A.D. 1400 to 1880 was chiefly based on indigenous gold mining organized by Ghanaians. These were generally Akan although they may have used labour from northern Ghana at times. Employing very laborious techniques and inadequate equipment, and constantly facing risk of loss of life, they nevertheless managed to produce the wealth which turned Ghana into a West African El Dorado, drew Europeans and western Sudanic peoples into the country, earned for it considerable reputation abroad and provided the metal basis for the magnificent regalia of the Akan courts.

Old Ghana had two faces. One face looked towards the middle Niger and Hausaland and the trans-Saharan caravan routes which linked West Africa with Roman and Islamic north Africa and north-east Africa. The other face looked southward towards the maritime coast, the scene of contact with the commercial representatives of several European nations. The Mande were the vital linkmen in the northern trade. The Akan were the chief entrepreneurs in the southern trade. The importance of long-range trade and its effect on society cannot be overstated. The gold trade, in particular, stimulated the process of urbanization and state formation in Ghana, especially in the gold mining areas of Akanland and along the trade routes leading northward and southward from the gold mining areas. The rise of Denkyira in the 16th century and Asante in the 17th century provides excellent illustration for this. Denkyira under the chiefs, Boadu Brempong and Ntim Gyakari, developed as a militarised state and carried out wars of territorial expansion against Assin, Adanse, Twifo, Wassa, Sefwi, Aowin and all south-west Ghana up to Axim coast. Denkyira's economic power which facilitated this imperial expansion was derived from the profits of the Begho-Jenne gold trade. Denkyiras and Adanses settled along this trade route and populous market centres like Bono Manso, Tafo, and Fomase grew along it. The Denkyira permitted the Oyoko peoples to settle in this area and channel some of the trade profits in return for the payment of annual tribute. The Denkyirahene, according to local traditions, became so rich that he never used the same gold ornament or regalia for more than one ceremonial occasion. His power was quite substantial and his *Mpintin* drums could say of his might: '*Kotoko som Amponsem*' – 'the Asante porcupine is subject to Amponsem of Denkyira'.

Smarting under this political and economic subservience to Denkyira, the Oyoko principalities formed an armed alliance and in two pitched battles at Adunku and Feyiase succeeded in shattering Denkyira power. The Asante went on to consolidate their military strength so that in the 18th and 19th centuries even British armies found them a force to reckon with. Probably never since the time of Mansa Musa of Mali had a West African state created such an impact in Europe as when Asante defeated a British army led by Sir Charles McCarthy in 1824. One factor was crucial in this era of militarisation and economic aggrandisement, namely, the introduction of guns and ammunition through the European maritime trade. Firearms were at once instrumental in territorial expansion, state building, in the acquisition of slaves for export, in commercial expansion and the protection of trade routes. The Denkyira war, together with the wars between Akyem and Akwamu and the many Asante wars which extended the frontiers of Asante roughly to the present-day boundaries of Ghana, were largely wars of trade and commercial imperialism. The trade in kola along the northeast route was no less important. This trade reached its height in the 19th century. Bowdich described the northeast trade route from Kumase to Salaga as 'one of the most beaten roads in Africa'. This trade promoted urbanization in northern Ghana. Eighteenth-century Salaga was a little Nanumba village. By 1817, with the decline of the trading centre of Kafaba, Salaga had become, in the words of Bowdich, 'the grand emporium of Gonja'. Dupuis likewise reported that Salaga had grown to become twice the size of Kumase. The exigencies of trade organization led to the establishment of administrative systems and bureaucracies in the kingdoms, not only among the Akan, but also among the Ga-Dangme peoples. The post of *Batahene*, head of the company of merchants, was well-known in the Akan civil service. In his book of 1602, Pieter de Marees provided illustrations of the *Batafo* of late 16th and early 17th century Elmina. Akan chiefs of the hinterland states are known to have stationed their representatives at the coastal towns to watch over their commercial interests. It was partly the demand for trade efficiency which led to the secularization of the theocratic principalities of the Accra coastlands.

Trade led to the development of new currencies. Iron (*narebuo*) was used as currency by the Akan of the Middle Iron Age. Recent research has shown that Akan use of gold dust as currency began in the pre-European period. Because the gold trade was pioneered along the northwest trade route with the Mande, it would appear that the Akan adopted the Islamic weight-system from the middle Niger area for weighing their gold. Although most Akan gold dealers weighed their gold at home before they went to the market, there grew up a group of professional men who carried scales (*futuo*) into the market and weighed gold for buyers. Pottery goldweights have been found in the Akan trading centre at ancient Begho, while one metal weight has been discovered in a 17th-century Akan funerary site at Twifo Heman.

Trade produced not only population increases but also population diversification. Mande Dyula communities from Mali were to be found in many towns of northern Ghana such as Buipe and Yagbum and also in the gold and kola entrepots of Brong and Kumase. There was a large Hausa migration into Dagomba and Gonja in the early 19th century. The *Qissat Salaga Tarikhu Gonja*, a 19th-century Arabic manuscript, states that as a result of a movement into Salaga of Arabs and Hausa from Katsina, Salaga became 'a town with a population of many races'. Bowdich and Meredith, both writing in the first quarter of the 19th century, spoke of a substantial Hausa migration into Kumase in the early 19th century.

A crucial factor in the evolution of Ghana was the advent of Europeans from 1471. A diversity of European peoples – Portuguese, French, Spanish, Dutch, English, Brandenburgers, Danes, and

Swedes – were attracted by prospects of trade into the country. For the first 400 years, their numbers were few, but when their function was transformed from traders to protectors and colonizers, their population, especially that of the British, increased. Three main phases of European commerce can be distinguished: an initial period based mainly on export of local goods accompanied by only brief temporary residence on the coast; a second period dominated by export of slaves; and a third period characterised mainly by export of 'legitimate goods' and accompanied by permanent residence and colonization both in the interior and the coast. When the Portuguese trade first began in the late 15th century, it was characterised chiefly by export of gold and ivory. At the very onset of the 16th century, Portuguese gold exports amounted to about 125 lbs weight per annum, but this soon increased to over 1500 lbs weight per annum. The Portuguese in return imported into the country new or second-hand textiles, hatchets, knives, beads, wine as well as a large quantity of brass vessels and bracelets, which were later melted down and re-cast by the local people. It was rumoured in Europe that the Portuguese had discovered rich gold mines on the West African coast. This produced something of a gold rush. The Portuguese governor of Elmina found himself as early as 1557 having to contend with French, Spanish and other European ships which 'glutted the whole coast with many goods of all kinds' in return for gold. From the 17th century to the early part of the 19th century when the slave trade was at its peak, the variety of exported goods doubled and the variety of imported goods quadrupled. By the late 17th century, for instance, the export list featured gold, ivory, hippo tusks, timber, animal skins, rice, salt (manufactured by the locals of Accra), and straw matting. The import list included brandy and wine, swords, daggers, knives, axe-heads, bars of iron, brass and iron bracelets, metal basins and jugs, leather products, old hats and caps, cloth both old and new, clay pipes and gun flints.

The European advent into Ghana had a considerable impact on the local situation initially on the coast and later in the hinterland. There is an element of truth in A. W. Lawrence's exaggerated view expressed in his book, *Trade Castles and Forts of West Africa* (1963, p. 29), that

> In all history there is nothing comparable with the effects produced by the forts of West Africa, nowhere else have small and transitory communities of traders so changed the life of the alien peoples who surround them, and indirectly of a vast region beyond.

Although the European nations were initially motivated primarily by commercial interests, they made important contributions as much towards the non-economic aspects of local life as towards the development and diversification of the subsistence and cash economy of the country. It was a great advantage that the Portuguese, who were the earliest pioneers of trade in West Africa, also had connections with the Mediterranean, with the Indian ocean area and with South America. For, from the early 16th century, they introduced into Ghana a variety of foreign foodcrops – lemons and melons from the Mediterranean area, maize, pineapples, pawpaws, sweet potatoes and groundnuts from America, a variety of yam from Asia and tobacco for smoking from

America. Subsequently, other nations added to the corpus of imported foodcrops – an abiding legacy to the modern Ghanaian economy. Another lasting trait bequeathed by Europe to Ghana was a *lingua franca*. Within a few years of the arrival of the Portuguese, some of the locals, particularly the boatmen, and those who provided services, or supplied fish, salt and other local materials, to European residents, acquired a working knowledge of Portuguese. When the Portuguese left, in 'Vicar of Bray' fashion, the people of each local town, depending on which European nationals resided in the local castle or fort, used Dutch or English as *lingua franca*. European writers such as Barbot observed that 17th-century Ghanaian seamen of Cape Coast and Elmina spoke English fluently. To this day, English has remained the *lingua franca* of Ghana. Some European words have become vernacularised into local languages, for instance, the Portuguese words, *asopatir* (shoe), *charta* (sheet), *pawpaw*, and *fetish*, the Dutch word *panis* (bread), the French words *l'adron* (rascal), *fenêtre* (window) and the English words *school* and *summons*.

Along with their languages, the Europeans bequeathed other traits to the local people – the European racial trait and European names – through inter-breeding with local women. Hence, the Ghanaian population includes fair-coloured, curly-haired mulatto people bearing foreign names such as Swanzy, Hesse, De Graft, Ribeiro, Riby-Williams, Hutton-Mills, Bannerman and Casely-Hayford. The European advent introduced a new religion and western style of education which have become the order of the day in modern Ghana. Although one room in Elmina castle was set aside for church functions as soon as the castle was built, King John II of Portugal built a separate church (the Church of St. George), where the Portuguese and their African converts and servants worshipped under the ministering of up to four chaplains. In the 17th century, the Dutch Reformed Church established a chaplaincy at Elmina Castle responsible for church activities. The Danes also established a chaplaincy but made it responsible for the running of an elementary school for mulatto children. At Cape Coast Castle, the English ran a similar school in the 18th century under the direction of a Ghanaian minister, Philip Quarque, trained by the Society for the Propagation of the Gospel. These were the fumbling beginnings of Christianity and western education.

To facilitate effective trade organization, to provide accommodation for resident Europeans and their servants and to protect them from the attacks of unfriendly locals or foreign interlopers, the European nations built fortified trading-stations. These took a variety of forms. The largest were known as 'castles', the medium-sized ones were called 'forts' and the small structures were described as 'lodges' (Map 10.1). However, there were other structures which defied classification, such as the structures attached to the 18th-century Dutch cotton plantations at Axim and Shama, the 18th-century Dutch sugar plantation and rum brewery at Butre and the 19th-century Danish plantation hill-resort at Kpomkpo, located thirty-two kilometres from Christiansborg. The first of these trading-stations was erected in 1482 by the Portuguese captain, Diego d'Azambuja, who called it 'the castle of St. George of the Mine'. Nearly all the building materials such as bricks, lime and stone used in the construction of Elmina castle (except for some local stone) were imported from Portugal. Originally, the castle was a two-storeyed building erected on a promontory in the style of a medieval European castle. It had a large outer fortified enclosure and a stronger, smaller inner enclosure also fortified. Inside there was a tall control-post tower. Sometime in the middle of the 16th century the castle was re-fortified and provided with strong bastions to conform with the style of Italian Renaissance castles which were more capable of withstanding heavy artillery fire than medieval castles. Subsequently, in the designing and building of other castles and forts in Ghana, the other European nations took their cue from the architectural style of Elmina castle and other Portuguese forts which in some respects bear resemblance to colonial forts and castles in America and the orient. But they made some modifications to the Portuguese style, for instance, there was a tendency to build one strongly fortified enclosure instead of two. Although most of the stone used in building these structures was obtained locally, the Dutch, English, Danish and Brandenburgers all tended to import from Europe nearly all the bricks and lime. It was in the great bastions of these trade-stations that slaves were kept while awaiting shipment across the Atlantic. Two-thirds of the number of European forts and castles built in West Africa were located on the coast of Ghana, which provides some indication of the extent of European commercial activities along this

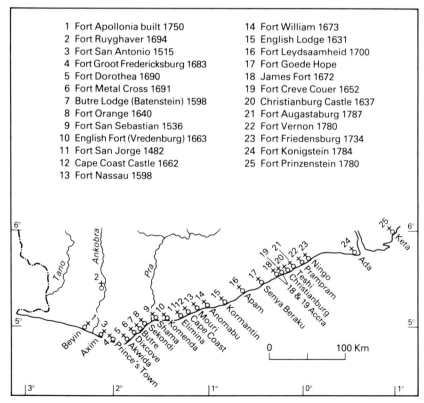

1 Fort Apollonia built 1750	14 Fort William 1673
2 Fort Ruyghaver 1694	15 English Lodge 1631
3 Fort San Antonio 1515	16 Fort Leydsaamheid 1700
4 Fort Groot Fredericksburg 1683	17 Fort Goede Hope
5 Fort Dorothea 1690	18 James Fort 1672
6 Fort Metal Cross 1691	19 Fort Creve Couer 1652
7 Butre Lodge (Batenstein) 1598	20 Christianburg Castle 1637
8 Fort Orange 1640	21 Fort Augastaburg 1787
9 Fort San Sebastian 1536	22 Fort Vernon 1780
10 English Fort (Vredenburg) 1663	23 Fort Friedensburg 1734
11 Fort San Jorge 1482	24 Fort Konigstein 1784
12 Cape Coast Castle 1662	25 Fort Prinzenstein 1780
13 Fort Nassau 1598	

Map 10.1 European castles, forts and lodges

stretch of the west coast. A number of extant castles and forts have been restored by the Ghana Museums and Monuments Board in recent times and are now used as museums, or administrative centres for the civil service or as rest houses (Fig. 10.1). They constitute the most striking visible legacy of Europe to Ghana. The original castle at Elmina has been modified several times by the Dutch and English, and more recently by the local administration, but the underground cistern built of imported bricks still survives – the oldest surviving European structure in tropical Africa.

Apart from the fortified buildings, the early Europeans also erected church buildings, ordinary domestic structures, and merchant or business houses outside the forts. In Elmina, for instance, some of the Portuguese lived in stone buildings in the township outside the castle. There are still extant in Accra, a Portuguese merchant's house built around 1600–1650 and a Danish merchant's house built around 1809. The idea of building in stone and in western architectural style quite appealed to the local people. Thus, some Ghanaians who had acquired wealth through trade and other activities built their own stone houses at Elmina, Cape Coast, Accra and other coastal towns. Between 1800 and 1930, the western architectural style in stone diffused into most parts of the country. The arcade art form which characterised the coastal castles and forts was reproduced in the chief's palace at Anum. The cult shrines which the Asante began constructing for use as traditional healing centres from the late 17th century onwards took on the elliptical arches represented in the coastal castle architecture. At the beginning of the present century, the advent of the Roman Catholic 'White Fathers' into northern Ghana led to the introduction of new architectural styles and materials. Thus when Navrongo Cathedral was built in 1920, some

Fig. 10.1 The Castle at Cape Coast built in 1662

Navrongo people soon put up two-storeyed indigenous buildings combining rectangular and circular features and other styles represented in the Cathedral.

The forts and castles have been the subject of extensive study by scholars from various disciplines – architecture, art history, trade history and archaeology. The most recent archaeological studies were undertaken by Bernard Golden and Merrick Posnansky, both of the University of Ghana. In 1969 to 1970, Golden carried out a reconnaissance survey of most of the extant fort sites, collected surface finds from within each fort area, as well as from the ruins of the local towns and villages which were located alongside the forts and castles. In a few cases, such as at Beyin, Golden carried out test excavations which produced local pottery, and European imported glass ware, beads, smoking pipes, cowry shells and pottery. Similarly, Merrick Posnansky's excavation in 1975 of the site of Fort Ruychaver, built by the Dutch in the interior to tap the gold resources of the Ankobra valley unearthed local pottery, imported pipes and beads and a large quantity of Dutch tiles used in the construction of the fort. There is clear evidence to suggest that the advent of the Europeans and the construction of the trade-stations, and their trade activities influenced the trend of development of local commerce, communications, business acumen, urbanization and culture in general. Among others, the published works of Towerson in the 16th century, de Marees and Barbot in the 17th century, Bosman in the 18th century and Bowdich and Meredith in the 19th century provide a general picture of a progressive growth of towns and population along the coast, though there is also evidence of a spell of urban depopulation, especially in the 18th century when the slave trade was at its peak. For instance, Elmina town was in 1486 declared a 'city' by the Portuguese who had encouraged its two villages to break off allegiance to their two local overlords and to form one independent city-state under Portuguese rule. By the 17th century, Barbot noted that Elmina had over a thousand stone houses and a population of about 6 000, while in the early 18th century Bosman noted that the town's population had decreased by about two-thirds. Meredith provides 19th century population estimates at 10 000 for Saltpond (Anomabu), 8 000 for Moure, 8 000 for Cape Coast, 4 000 for Winneba, 3 000 for Dixcove and 1 000 for Ada. The population of Accra oscillated in the 17th and 18th centuries, due as much to the emergence of the gold trading hinterland centre of Grand Accra (Ayawaso) to the detriment of the trading settlements of littoral Accra (comprising Socco, Apreg, Osu, and Labadi) as to the raids of the Akwamu. But Meredith estimated in 1812 that Little Accra had an army of about 1 000 which suggests a fairly large population.

The period after A.D. 1300 was one of marked cultural expansion and diversification, partly as a result of trade prosperity but also as part of the process of state formation and as a consequence of the advent of European and West African Sudanic peoples into Ghana. Just as the first European landfall off the Guinea coast in 1471 led to the building of Elmina castle and the subsequent spread of European building techniques and building materials along the coast and then into southern and middle Ghana, so the sack of Jenne, an important city-state on the Niger in 1473 led to the spread of Islamic religion, mosque architecture and Arabic literacy into northern Ghana and later, middle Ghana. Mande Dyula traders from Jenne who had waited for trade to come to them when Jenne was a free state, henceforth travelled along the trade paths in search of gold, ivory and salt. As they penetrated south they introduced into the Muslim quarters or *zongos* of the towns of north-western Ghana contemporary western Sudanic types of mosque. The fall of the Songhai empire which produced political instability in the middle Niger region at the end of the 16th century set in motion the Saghanughu movement which introduced more ideas of Islamic religion, architecture and education into Ghana.

It is no wonder therefore that separate studies undertaken in the 1960s by Oliver Davies of the University of Ghana and by J. T. Laube, Conservator of the Ghana Museums and Monuments Board, on the subject of Islamic monuments revealed that there are some 40 to 50 old mosques still extant in northern Ghana which date to various periods between A.D. 1500 and 1930. From the variety of mosque types, it is possible to classify the mosques on stylistic grounds and on the basis of the evidence of oral tradition into two groups, the 'Jenne' type and the 'Sudanic' type. The 'Jenne' type is a rectangular building with a flat roof surrounded by a parapet. Normally, it has only one tower and no buttresses. On the other hand, the 'Sudanic' type is characterised by a flat roof supported by a timber frame. It has a large number of buttresses around the exterior which project above the parapet and usually has two steeply pointed pyramidal towers. Over 80 per cent of the old mosques which have survived are of the 'Sudanic' type, and the extant 16th- and 17th-century mosques, such as those of Dawarape, Daboya and Larabanga, belong to the 'Sudanic' type. There is cor-roborative written evidence which supports the dating of these mosques by means of oral tradition. For instance, the Kitab Ghunja records the building of the mosque at Buipe in 1614/15. Some modern domestic houses located at the sites of the old mosques have protruding but-tresses, flat roofs and towerlike projections which indicate attempts to reproduce certain mosque features in domestic architecture.

An excellent illustration of the extent of Islamic and Sudanic influence in Ghana is the sharp contrast which exists between the palaces of the Ya Na of Yendi and the Wa Na of Wa. Both are palaces of paramount chiefs who have professed Islam since the 17th century, if not earlier; and both the Wala chieftains of Wa and the Yendi chieftains have a common Dagomba and Mamprussi ethnic origin. The palace of the Ya Na is in typical Dagomba architectural style. A Dagomba traditional compound has a central enclosure, ringed by circular huts which are linked together by walls and entered from outside through one reception hall. The central enclosure has one or more huts occupied by the head of the household. Important doorways are ornamented with an architrave of pottery set in the mud, in the fashion of medieval Islamic architectural ornamentation. The Ya Na's palace consists of seven such compounds of different sizes, each with a different function, but all very much like traditional Dagomba houses. On the other hand, the palace of the Wa Na is modelled on traditional western Sudanic architecture, with multi-buttresses protruding above the roof and decorative gables which usually feature at the entrances of the mosques.

Though the Wa Na's palace is much larger than the normal run of Sudanic mosques, its style is similar to that of the Sudanic mosque (Fig. 10.2).

Thanks to the territorial and commercial expansion of Asante in the 18th and 19th centuries along the northwest and northeast trade routes, elements of Islamic civilization began to percolate southward from northern Ghana and to help the development of Asante in matters political, economic and cultural. It is estimated that by the early 19th century there were over one thousand Muslims living in Kumase alone. The chief of Kumase Muslims around 1807 was Sheikh Baba Mohammed al Gamba from Mamprussi. As chief Imam, he led prayer and worship at the Kumase Friday mosque. As Qadi or Judge, he administered justice among the Muslims. As an educationist and scholar of Islamic learning, he opened and headed a school at Kumase where a large number of students including the household of the Asantehene joined in studying Islamic religion, Arabic language, and literature. Kumase became an international focus playing host to Muslims from Dagomba, Gonja, Hausaland, North Africa and the Near East. Muslims played an important role in the development of Asante economy and administration. Indeed, the correspondence of Asante political, diplomatic, social and economic affairs was conducted in Arabic. The 'Prime Minister' of Asante, the Gyasewahene, had a Muslim secretary, and the Asante civil service was manned by a number of Muslims. The Asantehene, Osei Kwame, tried – in the face of great opposition – to establish Koranic law as the civil code of Asante and tried to abolish certain traditional customs involving human sacrifice. King Osei Kwame and King Opoku II resettled Muslims from conquered lands of northern Ghana in Asante as a deliberate policy aimed at the Islamization of the kingdom. Today, Islam has spread into every region of Ghana. Detailed population studies by the Islam in Africa Project of the Christian Council of Ghana has shown that the vast majority of Muslims in Ghana are not in northern Ghana as would be expected, but are rather in the

Fig. 10.2 The Palace of the Wa Na (N. Ghana)

cities and large towns, especially, Accra, Kumase, Sekondi-Takoradi, Cape Coast, Tamale, and Sunyani. Islam and its associated culture have left their footprints in Ghana – the smock or *batakari* and cap, the Arabic language and script taught in Islamic schools and colleges and the Koranic religion and allied social customs. Above all, the mosque is the hallmark of Islamic culture in Ghana. From its minaret, the muezzin continues today to echo the words of over a thousand three hundred years of Islamic tradition:

Come to prayer, come to prayer;
Prayer is far more rewarding than sleep;
There is no god except God
And Muhammad is his prophet.

It seems that the greatest legacy of the past to modern Ghana lies in traditional culture, reference to which has been made already in regard to northern Ghana. The ancient Akan did not have writing in the conventional sense. It is not possible, therefore, to decipher with precision the trend of cultural development from the beginnings of the earliest Akan settlements till the European colonial period. From recent research, however, it is becoming increasingly clear that, fortunately for posterity, the earliest European officials, merchants and missionaries and their African disciples and servants failed to destroy the ancient culture of the Akan. Thus there is quite substantial evidence to demonstrate cultural continuity from the Middle Iron Age till the most recent times in metal technology, the arts and crafts. It has already been demonstrated that wooden stools, the thrones of modern local chiefs, served the same purpose when the earliest Europeans arrived on the coast. Joao de Barros, Towerson, Pieter de Marees, Bosman and Barbot made reference to the political function of stools among the coastal Akan. It was no different further inland. A Danish envoy to Kumase in the middle of the 18th century reported (F. L. Romer, 1760, p. 191):

The Asantehene's throne is a golden nugget, which eight men have to carry out and in with a rope tied round it and poles through it.

It is thought that the Asantehene's wooden stool gilded with gold leaf may be a copy of the original throne of pure gold dating back to the late 17th century. State swords which are Akan instruments for enstoolment of chiefs, for taking oaths of office, and the staffs of office of envoys sent on royal errands are pre-European in origin. They were described by Pieter de Marees, Muller, Bosman and Barbot as well as Bowdich. The Asante raised the manufacture of state swords to a fine art in the 19th and early 20th century when it became the custom of every Asante king to make state swords whose scabbards were decorated with elegant gold ornaments called *abosodee* cast by the *cire perdue* method in the form of figurative or proverbial sculptures, symbolising royal wealth and power. Herbert Cole and Doran Ross, who have studied not only the literature on the subject but extant examples dating to between the 17th century and the early 20th century, wrote (in the *Arts of Ghana*, 1977) of the state swords with *abosodee* ornamentation that they constitute 'the most spectacular products of the Akan goldsmith art'. Linguist staffs, or the staffs of office of the *Okyeame* or chief spokesman of the king's court, were described by Mueller in the middle of the 17th century: although earlier references are hard to come by, there is no reason to believe that the staff of the *obcjammi*, as Mueller described him, was a foreign importation. The same may be said of other important musical instruments used at the royal court, namely the ivory trumpet or *ntahera* and the iron gong. Indeed, the Portuguese writer, Pina, wrote of the Elmina King, Caramansa: 'Hither the king came and before him a great noise of bugles, bells and horns.' The designs and symbols of *kente* and *adinkra* cloths which are world-famous are an indigenous heritage *par excellence* handed down the generations. It is clear that ·behind these purely physical aspects of culture, technology and art, was a rich background of profound philosophy and wisdom and that Akan philosophy and technology blended to form a verbal art which has survived into modern times – a priceless legacy. In Ghana today, the national radio and television network starts its daily news broadcasts with an invitation in the surrogate or symbolic form of language expressed musically through the talking drum and the gong. The crests of the universities in Ghana and many other institutions and associations, the symbols of many learned journals and publications, the state of Ghana coat of arms and regalia all depict Akan proverbial and philosophical symbols, some of which are also recorded in archaeological data and historical monuments.

The ancient Akan legacy has come down not only to modern non-Akan Ghanaians but also to some neighbouring West African peoples and even further to the New World. J. H. Kwabena Nketia, the world's leading exponent of African musicology asserts (1973, p. 81):

> Asante, the last of the successive Akan kingdoms which emerged as powerful political states in Ghana in the pre-colonial era had a large sphere of influence which extended into northern and southern Ghana, to the borders of the Ivory Coast and Dahomey. As a result of this, there are Asante *atumpan* talking drums in Dagomba, Mamprussi, Gonja, and Wala areas of northern Ghana, which are played in Asante style with Asante texts as the basis. Songs in Akan are performed in non-Akan areas among the Ga and the Ewe.

The Dahomean orchestra called *kantanto* was borrowed from Asante. Similarly, the Akofin trumpet ensemble of Dahomey is a direct descendant of the Nkofe trumpet ensemble of Asante introduced by King Osei Kwadwo (1764–77) after his predecessor Kusi Obodum had sent a mission to Dahomey. King Osei Tutu according to oral traditions, introduced the Asante *Kete* flute and drum orchestra into Dahomey where it assumed the name *Kpete honu* or *Blou Kpete*. As a result of trade and cultural contact, Akan cultural traits from Ghana are found in the Ivory Coast. Akan gold weights with identical symbolism and styles are found among the Abron, Anyi, Atie, Ebrie and Baoule of the Ivory Coast. In the town of Erebou near Bondoukou, in the Ivory Coast, there is a king of Gyaman whose court exhibits nearly all the characteristics of the

Akan court of Brong Ahafo. The Erebou chief himself speaks Akan in private but speaks the local Ivory Coast language at public functions.

Akan culture was transplanted through the slave trade into the New World. Wherever slaves of Akan origin had the opportunity they revived Akan culture of Ghana. The maroons or 'bush negroes' of Surinam, the maroons of Haiti, Jamaica, Santo Domingo, South Georgia and the Gulla Islands provide illustrations of transplanted Akan culture in the New World. Roger Bastide, writing in *Les Ameriques Noires* (1967, English trans., p. 11–12) states:

> It is, above all, among the Bush Negroes of Dutch and French Guiana that we find Fanti-Ashanti Gold Coast culture in its purest form . . . in terms of language, masks, folk lore, art, magic, religion, institutions, social organization, economic life and technology.

The naming custom using the list of 'day-names', as applicable among the Akan of Ghana, is exactly paralleled in the Guianas as follows:

		Name
Day	Guiana	Ghana
Monday	Couachi	Kwasi
Tuesday	Codio	Kojo
Wednesday	Couamina	Kwamena
Thursday	Couacou	Kweku
Friday	Yao	Yao
Saturday	Cofi	Kofi
Sunday	Couami	Kwame

(R. Bastide, 1967, English trans., p. 56)

Among the 18th-century Gullahs of Carolina, the names of African slaves (e.g. Abonna, Quamana and Quash) followed the Akan naming system. Bastide notes that in Jamaica the worship of Akan *Onyame*, the ancestors, and the Kormanti cult worship have been recorded, and that Miss Nancy, the trickster, who features in Jamaican folktales is none other than the clever trickster, Kweku Ananse or the spider of Akan unwritten fictional narratives. Peter Hammond observes in an article entitled 'West Africa and the Afro-Americans' in *The African Experience* (ed. by Paden and Soja, p. 205):

> In parts of the forest regions of the Guianas where escaped slaves from the Dutch and French owned plantations fled into the interior and re-established an essentially West African pattern of life, West African oral literary traditions were retained in almost pure form. Characteristic West African tales such as the ones concerning the spider Trickster, 'Anansi' continue to be told with most elements of their original narrative style and plot intact.

Akan music and dance has similarly found its way into American negro culture. M. J. Herskovits, who has researched intensively into the subject of Ghanaian Akan survivals in the New World, wrote in *The Myth of the Negro Past* (1941, p. 146):

> On the basis of uncontrolled observation, it is a common place that many American negro forms of dancing are essentially African; and this is confirmed by motion pictures taken of the Kwaside rites for the ancestors of the chief of the Ashanti village of Asokore, which include a perfect example of the Charleston.

Traditional hair styles which are derivatives of Akan hairstyles and their proverb-names have been recorded in Dutch Guiana and the West Indies. After field research in the old British Guiana, Dutch Guiana, and the West Indies and comparisons with Rattray's field notes on the Akan, M. J. Herskovits concluded in his article 'Wari in the New World' (*Journal of Royal Anthropological Institute*, vol. 62, 1932):

> This form of the game – the 'Djuku Langa' type of Dutch Guiana, the 'Awari' of the Guiana coastal region and the 'English Wari' of the English-speaking islands – has come directly from the Gold Coast.

In St. Lucia, the Akan yam festival has been observed annually among the negroes. In Barbados, Asante funeral customs have been observed in recent times.

The ancient Akan, like other ethnic groups in Ghana, borrowed much from the outside world to build the edifice of their civilization. But no one can contest the fact that they have also influenced the evolution of some cultures in West Africa and in the New World, and so made a contribution, however small, to world civilization.

Appendix

Radiocarbon dates from Ghana

(Dates quoted are based on half life of 5568 years)

Abbreviations

A.Q.   *Africa Quarterly*
B.I.A.S.   *Bulletin of Institute of African Studies,* Legon, Ghana.
J.A.H.   *Journal of African History,* Cambridge, U.K.
N.A.   *Nyame Akuma,* Calgary, Canada.
P.P.S.   *Proceedings of the Prehistoric Society,* Cambridge, U.K.
SAN.   *Sankofa, Legon Journal of Archaeological and Historical
            Studies,* Legon, Ghana.
W.A.A.N.   *West African Archaeological Newsletter,* Ibadan, Nigeria.
W.A.J.A.   *West African Journal of Archaeology,* Ibadan, Nigeria.
W.A.T.P.   *West African Trade Project Report,* Legon, Ghana.

Site	Context	Date	Serial no.	Reference
Jimam	'Guinea Aterian'	10 450 ± 300 B.C.	I-2264	W.A.J.A., I, 1971
Lake Bosumtwi	Holocene high lake level	7 930 ± 220 B.C.	GIF-3660	SAN. 2, 1976
Gao Lagoon	Late Stone Age	4 190 ± 95 B.C.	N-3212	N.A., 14, 1979
Gao Lagoon	Later Stone Age (with pottery)	3 900 ± 80 B.C.	N-2982	N.A., 14, 1979
Nalori (Limbisi)		3 880 ± 115 B.C.	I-2265	W.A.J.A., I, 1971
Takoradi	Late Holocene marine transgression	3 880 ± 70 B.C.	GRO-1194	W.A.A.N., 10, 1968
Bosumpra Rockshelter	Later Stone Age	3 420 ± 100 B.C.	N-1805	P.P.S., 41, 1965
Bosumpra Rockshelter	Later Stone Age	3 260 ± 100 B.C.	N-1803	J.A.H., 17, 1976
Nalori (Limbisi)		3 070 ± 105 B.C.	I-2266	W.A.J.A., I, 1971
Gao Lagoon	Shell midden	2 230 ± 140 B.C.	GIF-4241	N.A., XI, 1977
Ntereso	Kintampo culture	1 630 ± 130 B.C.	SR-52	J.A.H., 8, 1967
Kintampo (K6)	Bwihweili phase	1 620 ± 84 B.C.	BIRM-29	B.I.A.S., 4, 1968
Kintampo (K1)	Kintampo culture	1 610 ± 100 B.C.	I-2698	W.A.A.N., 8, 1968
Kintampo (K1)	Pumpun phase	1 580 ± 100 B.C.	I-2699	B.I.A.S., 4, 1968
Mumute	Kintampo culture	1 500 ± 110 B.C.	N-1984	J.A.H., 17, 1976
Kintampo (K8)	Pumpun phase	1 451 ± 75 B.C.	BIRM-31	B.I.A.S., 4, 1968
Kintampo (K1)	Pumpun phase	1 389 ± 35 B.C.	BIRM-30	B.I.A.S., 4, 1968
Ntereso	Kintampo culture	1 320 ± 100 B.C.	SR-81	J.A.H., 10, 1969
Kintampo (K1)	Kintampo culture	1 270 ± 110 B.C.	I-2697	B.I.A.S., 4, 1968
Ntereso	Kintampo culture	1 240 ± 120 B.C.	SR-61	J.A.H., 8, 1967
Lake Bosumtwi	Present lake level	570 ± 200 B.C.	GIF-3651	SAN. 2, 1976
Tema	Early Iron Age	100 ± 90 B.C.	GIF-1676	J.A.H., 17, 1976
Kintampo	Upper level	57 ± 68 B.C.	BIRM-28	W.A.J.A., 4, 1974
Daboya	Lower level	50 ± 140 B.C.	GX-6133	N.A., 15, 1979
Lake Bosumtwi	Present lake level	A.D. 10 ± 300	GIF-3652	SAN. 2, 1976
Ntereso	Upper Level	A.D. 60 ± 110	SR-90	J.A.H., 10, 1969
Kpone	Early Iron Age	A.D. 150 ± 75	N-3213	N.A., 14, 1979
Hani	Iron Age slag mound	A.D. 180 ± 75	N-2140	J.A.H., 17, 1976
Paradise Beach	Shore lines	A.D. 320 ± 90	GIF-1675	J.A.H., 17, 1976
Abam (Bono)	Iron Age slag mound	A.D. 320 ± 30	BLN-1730	N.A., 10, 1977

Site	Description	Date	Lab no.	Reference
Amuowi I	Rockshelter	A.D. 440 ± 70	N-1801	J.A.H., 17, 1976
Bonoso	Iron Age settlement	A.D. 750 ± 90	N-2343	SAN, 2, 1976
Daboya	Lower level	A.D. 770 ± 165	GX-6134	N.A., 15, 1979
New Buipe	Iron Age mound Phase 2	A.D. 780 ± 100	I-2702	W.A.J.A., I, 1971
New Buipe	Iron Age mound Phase 2	A.D. 790 ± 100	I-2701	W.A.J.A., I, 1971
Bonoso	Iron Age settlement	A.D. 1005 ± 80	N-2344	SAN, 2, 1976
Namasa	Iron Age settlement	A.D. 1019 ± 158	BIRM-75	W.A.J.A., I, 1971
Begho	Nyarko quarter	A.D. 1045 ± 80	N-2142	J.A.H., 17, 1976
Begho	Nyarko quarter	A.D. 1120 ± 80	N-2141	J.A.H., 17, 1976
Daboya	Middle level	A.D. 1180 ± 150	GX-6132	N.A., 15, 1979
Bosumpra	Rockshelter, Upper level	A.D. 1200 ± 75	N-1804	J.A.H., 17, 1976
Bono Manso	Iron Age, Phase I	A.D. 1235 ± 75	N-2493	Unpub. thesis
Namasa	Iron Age settlement	A.D. 1243 ± 92	BIRM-154	W.A.J.A., I, 1971
Akyekyemabuo	Rockshelter	A.D. 1265 ± 75	N-1961	J.A.H., 17, 1976
Namasa	Iron Age settlement	A.D. 1299 ± 95	BIRM-80	W.A.J.A., I, 1971
Bono Manso	Iron Age, Phase I	A.D. 1380 ± 75	N-1803	J.A.H., 17, 1976
Ladoku	Cherekecherete phase	A.D. 1400 ± 75	N-2968	N.A., 15, 1979
Dapaa	Iron Age slag mound I	A.D. 1400 ± 100	GX-4226	SAN, 2, 1976
Begho	Brong Quarter Site I	A.D. 1430 ± 100	N-930	A.Q., XI, 1971
New Buipe	Iron Age, Phase 3	A.D. 1445 ± 100	I-2700	W.A.J.A., I, 1971
Begho	Brong Quarter Site I	A.D. 1450 ± 100	N-932	A.Q., XI, 1971
Begho	Brong Quarter Site 2	A.D. 1450 ± 100	N-1438	W.A.T.P., 2, 1976
Juni	Iron Age mound	A.D. 1460 ± 125	I-3152	W.A.J.A., I, 1971
Dapaa	Iron Age slag mound I	A.D. 1480 ± 65	N-2286	SAN, 2, 1976
Akyem Manso	Iron Age earthworks	A.D. 1485 ± 65	N-2208	SAN, 2, 1976
New Buipe	Iron Age, Phase 3	A.D. 1495 ± 95	I-2705	W.A.J.A., I, 1971
New Buipe	Iron Age, Phase 3	A.D. 1495 ± 95	I-2706	W.A.J.A., I, 1971
Akyem Manso	Iron Age earthworks	A.D. 1510 ± 80	N-2207	SAN, 2, 1976
Begho	Dwinfuo Quarter Site 3	A.D. 1520 ± 75	N-2288	SAN, 2, 1976
Bono Manso	Iron Age, Phase I	A.D. 1520 ± 30	BLN-1728	N.A., 10, 1977
Bono Manso	Iron Age, Phase I	A.D. 1520 ± 75	N-2490	Unpub. thesis
New Buipe	Iron Age	A.D. 1530 ± 95	I-3740	W.A.J.A., I, 1971

Site	Context	Date	Serial no.	Reference
New Buipe	Iron Age	A.D. 1540 ± 90	I-2704	W.A.J.A., 1, 1971
Begho	Brong Quarter Site 2	A.D. 1550 ± 95	GX-2030	A.Q., XI, 1971
Bono Manso	Iron Age, Phase 1	A.D. 1585 ± 70	N-2629	Unpub. thesis
Begho	Dwinfuo, Quarter Site 3	A.D. 1595 ± 60	N-2287	SAN., 2, 1976
Ahwene Koko	Wenchi capital site	A.D. 1595 ± 80	N-2345	SAN., 2, 1976
Amuowi	Phase 2	A.D. 1610 ± 80	N-1802	J.A.H., 17, 1976
Bono Manso	Late Iron Age, Phase 1	A.D. 1615 ± 70	N-2628	Unpub. thesis
Buroburo	Top level overlying Kintampo culture	A.D. 1620 ± 50	R-133	SAN., 2, 1976
Juni	Iron Age mound	A.D. 1630 ± 85	I-3119	W.A.J.A., 1, 1971
Kebitokebombe	Iron Age mound	A.D. 1630 ± 95	I-3737	W.A.J.A., 1, 1971
Bono Manso	Phase 2	A.D. 1635 ± 30	BLN-1729	N.A., 10, 1977
New Buipe	Iron Age mound	A.D. 1640 ± 90	I-2703	W.A.J.A., 1, 1971
Dapaa	Iron Age slag, mound 2	A.D. 1650 ± 95	GX-4227	SAN., 2, 1976
Ladoku	La Phase	A.D. 1660 ± 80	N-2969	N.A., 15, 1979
Begho	Brong Quarter Site 1	A.D. 1665 ± 100	N-931	A.Q., XI, 1971
Kitare	Earthworks	Older than 1665	I-2530	W.A.J.A., 1, 1971
Ladoku	La Phase	A.D. 1680 ± 80	N-3346	N.Y., 15, 1980
Kebitokebombe	Iron Age mound	A.D. 1680 ± 95	I-3738	W.A.J.A., 1, 1971
Kitare	Earthworks	A.D. 1705 ± 125	I-2531	W.A.J.A., 1, 1971
Bono Manso	Phase 3	A.D. 1710 ± 75	N-2491	Unpub. thesis
Begho	Brong Quarter Site 1	A.D. 1710 ± 100	N-929	A.Q., XI, 1971
Akyem Manso	Earthworks	A.D. 1740 ± 115	N-2206	SAN., 2, 1976
Buroburo	Top level overlying Kintampo culture	A.D. 1740 ± 50	R-134	SAN., 2, 1976
Kitare	Earthworks	A.D. 1745 ± 100	I-2532	W.A.J.A., 1, 1971
Bono Manso	Phase 3	A.D. 1760 ± 40	BLN-1731	N.A., 10, 1977
Apreku	Rockshelter, Upper level	A.D. 1765 ± 75	N-1964	J.A.H., 17, 1976
Ladoku	La Phase	A.D. 1785 ± 70	N-2970	N.A., 15, 1979
Apreku	Rockshelter, Upper level	A.D. 1790 ± 70	N-1962	J.A.H., 17, 1976
Apreku	Rockshelter, Upper level	A.D. 1825 ± 60	N-1963	J.A.H., 17, 1976

Select bibliography and suggestions for further reading

Published works

ABRAHAM, W., *The Mind of Africa*, London, 1967.

ANTUBAM, K., *Ghana's heritage of culture*, Leipzig, 1963.

ASIWAJU and CROWDER (eds.), 'The African Diaspora', *Tarikh*, 5, 2, 1978.

BARBOT, J., *A Description of the Coasts of North and South Guinea*, in Churchill, *Collection of Voyages and Travels*, London, 1732.

BASTIDE, R., *African Civilizations in the New World*, Harper & Row, 1971.

BLAKE, J. W., *Europeans in West Africa 1450–1560*, Hakluyt Society, London, 1942.

BOAHEN, A. A., 'Who are the Akan?', *Actes du Colloque inter-universitaire, Ghana–Cote d'Ivoire*, Abidjan, 1974.

BOSMAN, W., *A New and Accurate Description of the Coast of Guinea*, London, 1705.

BOWDICH, T. E., *Mission from Cape Coast Castle to Ashantee*, London, 1819.

BRIAN WILLS, J., (ed.), *Agriculture and Land Use in Ghana*, London, 1962.

CALVOCORESSI, D. S., and YORK, R. N., 'The State of Archaeological Research in Ghana', *West African Journal of Archaeology*, Vol. 1, 1971.

COLE, H. and ROSS, D., *The Arts of Ghana*, Los Angeles, 1977.

DAPPER, O., *Africa – being an accurate description of the region*, in Ogilby, J., London, 1670.

DAVIES, O., *The Quaternary in the Coastlands of Guinea*, Glasgow, 1964.

DAVIES, O., *West Africa before the Europeans*, London, 1967.

DE MAREES, PIETER, *A Description and Historical Declaration of the Golden Kingdom of Guinea*, Glasgow, 1604.

DODDS, M., (ed.) *History of Ghana*, Accra, 1974.

DOLPHYNE, F., 'The Languages of the Ghana Ivory Coast border', *Actes du colloque inter-universitaire Ghana – Cote d'Ivoire,* Abidjan, 1974.

DOMBROWSKI, J. C., 'Mumute and Bonoase, two sites of the Kintampo industry', *Sankofa,* volume 2, 1976.

DOMBROWSKI, J. C., 'Earliest settlements in Ghana and Kintampo industry', in *Proceedings of 7th Pan-African Congress on Prehistory,* Nairobi, 1977.

DARK, P. J. C., *Bush Negro Art, an African art in the Americas,* London, 1954.

DUPUIS, J., *Journal of a Residence in Ashantee,* London, 1824.

EPHSON, I. S., *Ancient Forts and Castles of the Gold Coast (Ghana),* Accra, 1970.

FAGE, J. D., *Ghana: a Historical Interpretation,* Wisconsin University Press, 1959.

FLIGHT, C., 'The Kintampo culture and its place in the economic prehistory of West Africa', in Harlan, De Wet and Stemmler (eds.), *Origins of African Plant Domestication,* London, 1976.

FYNN, J. K., *Asante and its Neighbours,* London, 1971.

GARRARD, T., *Akan Goldweights and the Gold Trade,* London, 1980.

HERSKOVITS, M. J., 'The Negro in the New World', *American Anthropology,* volume 32, 1930.

HYLAND, A., 'An Introduction to the Traditional and Historical Architecture of Ghana', in M. Dodds (ed.), *History of Ghana,* Accra, 1974.

JUNNER, N. R., 'Gold in the Gold Coast', *Geological Survey: Report of the Gold Coast,* Mem. No. 4, Accra, 1935.

KILSON, M., *Kpele Lala, Ga Religious Songs and Symbols,* Harvard University Press, 1971.

KROPP-DAKUBU, M. E., 'Linguistic prehistoric and historical reconstruction of the Ga-Dangbe migrations', *Transactions of Historical Society of Ghana,* vol. 13, 1976.

KROPP-DAKUBU, M. E., 'On the Linguistic geography of the area of ancient Begho', in H. Trutenau (ed.), *Communications from the Basel Africa Bibliography,* 4, 1976.

LAWRENCE, A. W., *Trade Castles and Forts of West Africa,* London, 1963.

MAUNY, R., *Tableau Geographique de l'Ouest Africain au Moyen Age,* IFAN, Dakar, 1961.

MAUNY, R., *Les Siècles Obscurs de l'Afrique Noire,* Nancy, 1964.

MIEGE, J., 'Les Cultures Vivrières en Afrique Occidentale', *Cahiers d'Outre Mer,* volume 7, 1954.

MUELLER, W. J., *Die Africanische auf der Guineischen Gold Coast gelegene landschafft Fetu*, Hamburg, 1973.

NKETIA, J. H. K., 'Historical Evidence in Ga Religious Music', in Vansina, Mauny and Thomas (eds.), *The Historian in Tropical Africa*, Oxford, 1959.

NKETIA, J. H. K., 'Music in Ghana', in *Proceedings of Fifth International Congress of Africanists*, Accra, 1967.

NKETIA, J. H. K., 'The Musician in Akan Society', *The Traditional Artist in African Societies,* W. L. Azeredo (ed.), Indiana University Press, 1973.

OZANNE, P. C., 'Ghana', in P. L. Shinnie (ed.) *The Iron Age of Africa*, Oxford, 1971.

PACHECO PEREIRA, D., *Esmeraldo de Situ orbis*, G. M. T. Kimble (ed.), London, 1937.

POSNANSKY, M., *Discovering Ghana's Past*, Accra, 1971.

POSNANSKY, M., 'Archaeology, Technology and Akan Civilisation', *Journal of African Studies*, volume 2, 1975.

POSNANSKY, M., New Radiocarbon Dates from Ghana, *Sankofa*, vol. 2, 1976.

POSNANSKY, M. and McKINTOSH, R., 'New Radiocarbon Dates for Northern and Western Africa', *Journal of African History*, vol. 17, 1976.

PRUSSIN, L., *Architecture in Northern Ghana*, Berkeley, 1969.

RATTRAY, R. S., *Ashanti*, Oxford, 1923.

RATTRAY, R. S., *Religion and Art in Ashanti*, Oxford, 1927.

RØMER, F. L., *Tilforladelig Efterretning orn Kysten Guinea,* Copenhagen, 1760.

SHAW, T., *Excavation at Dawu*, Edinburgh, 1961.

SHAW, T., 'The Prehistory of West Africa', in J. F. Ajayi and M. Crowder (eds.), *History of West Africa*, London, 1971.

SMIT, A. F. J., 'Ghana and its Geology', in M. Dodds (ed.), *History of Ghana*, Legon, 1974.

SWITHENBANK, M., *Ashanti Fetish Houses*, Accra, 1969.

TILLEMAN, E., *En liden Enfolding beretning on det Landskab Guinea og dets beskaffenhed,* Copenhagen, 1697.

TODD, LORD, *Problems of the Technological Society*, Accra, 1973.

TRUTENAU, H. M. J., *Languages of the Akan Area*, Basel, 1976.

WARD, W. E. F., *A History of Ghana*, London, 1958.

VAN DEN BROECKE, P., *Reisen Naar West–Afrika 1605–1614*, Ratelband (ed.), 1950.

WILD, R. P., 'The Inhabitants of the Gold Coast and Ashanti before the Akan Invasion', *Gold Coast Teachers' Journal*, vol. 6–7, 1934–35.

WILKS, I., 'The Mossi and Akan states A.D. 1500–1800', in J. F. Ajayi and M. Crowder, *History of West Africa*, London, 1975.

WILKS, I., *Asante in the 19th century*, Cambridge, 1975.

WOLFSON, F., *Pageant of Ghana*, London, 1958.

Cyclostyled monographs and reports

DAVIES, O., Ghana Field Notes, Legon:

> 1970, Part I – Togo;
> 1970, Part II – Northern Ghana;
> 1972, Part III – Ashanti;
> 1976, Part IV – Southern Ghana.
> Excavation at Ntereso, Pietermaritzburg (1973).
> Excavation at Ahinsan, Legon (1977).

DAAKU, K. Y., Oral Traditions of Adanse, Legon (1971).

FYNN, J. K., Oral Traditions of the Fante (Parts 1 to 4), Legon, (1975–77).

POSNANSKY, M., West African Trade Project (Begho excavations), Part I, Legon (1973).

POSNANSKY, M., West African Trade Project (Begho excavations), Part III, Legon (1976).

Unpublished theses

AGORSAH, E. K., 'The Prehistory of the Begho area', M.A., Legon, 1975.

ANQUANDAH, J. R., 'Cultural Developments in Western Africa in the light of Pottery Studies', M. Litt., Oxford, 1967.

BELLIS, J. O., 'Archaeology and the Culture History of the Akan of Ghana', Ph.D., Indiana, U.S.A., 1972.

BOACHIE-ANSAH, J., 'Archaeological Contribution to Wenchi History', M.A., Legon, 1978.

CROSSLAND, L. B., 'Archaeology of the Begho area', M.A., Legon, 1973.

EFFAH GYAMFI, K., 'Bono Manso – an archaeological investigation into early Akan urbanism', Ph.D., Legon, 1978.

KENSE, F. J., 'Daboya: A Gonja Frontier', Ph.D., Calgary, Canada, 1981.

KIYAGA-MULINDWA, 'The Archaeology of the Earthworks of Akim-Manso', M.A. John Hopkins, U.S.A., 1976.

MCINTOSH, R., 'The Archaeology and Ethnography of Architecture at Hani (Begho)', M. Litt, Cambridge, 1975.

MUSONDA, F. B., 'Archaeology of the Late Stone Age along the Voltaian Scarp', M. A., Legon, 1976.

ODOTEI, I., 'The Ga and their Neighbours', Ph.D., Legon, 1972.

Index